THE
MIND/BODY
EFFECT

*How Behavioral Medicine Can Show
You the Way to Better Health*

HERBERT BENSON, M.D.

SIMON AND SCHUSTER · NEW YORK

Published by Simon and Schuster
A Division of Gulf & Western Corporation
Simon & Schuster Building
Rockefeller Center
1230 Avenue of the Americas
New York, New York 10020
Illustrations by Jerome Reicher,
Arrco Medical Art and Design, Inc.
Designed by Edith Fowler
Manufactured in the United States of America

1 2 3 4 5 6 7 8 9 10

Library of Congress Cataloging in Publication Data

Benson, Herbert.
  The mind/body effect.

  Bibliography: p.
  1. Medicine and psychology. 2. Mind and body.
I. Title.
R726.5.B46   616′.001′9   78–13543
ISBN 0–671–24143–5

TO JENNIFER AND GREGORY

FOREWORD

FOR MORE than a decade, my primary research interests have focused upon bridging the disciplines of medicine, physiology, psychology and psychiatry. As a result of these interests, I am convinced that many aspects of the teaching, research and practice of modern medicine can be altered to provide you with better health care. To facilitate the teaching of these concepts, a Behavioral Medicine course has been initiated at Harvard Medical School. A Division of Behavioral Medicine Section has been formed at Boston's Beth Israel Hospital to continue collaborative research in this area and to apply these principles to the care of patients. One of the major tenets of the teaching and practice of Behavioral Medicine is that individuals must assume more responsibility for their own health care. Your health is both your responsibility and that of your physician; it is a two-way proposition.

My hope is that this book will provide a new perspective which will allow you and members of the medical profession to interact better. This book was not written to give specific medical advice concerning personal health care. However, you must understand what can reasonably be expected from medicine. You can adopt a more effective approach to health care by taking an historical perspective. A proper balance between traditional and modern medical practices is necessary so that people can remain well for as long as possible and receive optimal treatment when ill. Without this proper balance, more individuals might become like the woman cited in the Gospel according to St. Mark, "who had suffered much under many physicians, and had spent all that she had, and was no better, but rather grew worse."

Since Behavioral Medicine is still evolving, it may be viewed differently by others. For those of my colleagues already working in Behavioral Medicine, I trust that this book will be considered as an attempt to advance an important mutual endeavor. A term other than "Behavioral Medicine" might have been used: "Holistic Health," "Holistic Medicine," "Wholistic Health," "Integral Medicine" and "Humanistic Medicine" are similar approaches.

Almost all the case histories presented in this book have been reported in the medical literature. No examples of my own patients have been cited unless written, informed consent was received.

I have not consistently eliminated the sole use of the male gender when referring to individuals. An excess of the awkward phrases, "his or hers," "she or he," "her or him," would have resulted. I apologize to those who might be offended.

I am indebted to the many investigators and observers who have contributed to the literature concerned with health and disease. Whenever possible, I have acknowledged their contributions in the text.

I gratefully thank Karen D. Crassweller, Jamie B.

8

Kotch and Patricia A. Arns for their superb assistance in the research, development and preparation of this book. I also thank Nancy E. MacKinnon for her interest and excellent secretarial assistance. I acknowledge the contributions of Mark D. Epstein and Martha M. Greenwood, who indirectly aided this book by working on related research projects. For their counsel, I thank David M. Roseman and Carl R. Croce. I am ever indebted to my wife, Marilyn, for her honest, direct and unerringly sound judgments as well as for her patience and support.

Significant aspects of the book were made possible through funds donated in memory of the late Joel Cheney Wells by Mr. and Mrs. Frank M. Brennan. I also gratefully acknowledge the support of Robert L. Allen and William K. Coors. I hope that this book will help to fulfil their faith in the future of Behavioral Medicine. The research and development of the book were also funded, in part, by the following grants from the United States Public Health Service: RR-01032 from the General Clinical Research Centers' Program of Research Resources, HL10539 and MH25101.

1

EVERY AGE seems to look back fondly at previous generations. More than 4600 years ago, the legendary Yellow Emperor of China asked his divinely inspired teacher, Ch'i Po:

> I have heard that in ancient times the people lived [through the years] to be over a hundred years, and yet they remained active and did not become decrepit in their activities. But nowadays people reach only half of that age and yet become decrepit and failing. Is it because the world changes from generation to generation? Or is it because mankind is becoming negligent [of the laws of nature]?

His teacher answered:

> In ancient times those people who understood [the way of self-cultivation] ... lived in harmony with the arts of divination.

There was temperance in eating and drinking. Their hours of rising and retiring were regular and not disorderly and wild. By these means the ancients kept their bodies united with their souls, so as to fulfill their allotted span completely, measuring unto a hundred years before they passed away.

Our current and more accurate data argue against the concept that previous generations lived longer. We now not only live longer than ever before, but also, through the benefits of modern medicine, enjoy healthier lives. Yet many are still not satisfied with their state of health. Disenchanted with the medical profession, people seek help from various organizations and cults which promise relief from their problems. People also seek health advice from a myriad of books which instruct them what to eat and not to eat, how to exercise, how to relax and how to behave. Why is it that people do not have more faith in the present medical system and turn to it for advice, since medicine has achieved many, truly remarkable advances?

The scientific and medical advances themselves are causing medicine to move away from some of your most basic needs. As our modern technological society developed, time-tested approaches were considered to be unscientific and "old fashioned." By adopting an historical perspective, I will show that medicine has made use of worthwhile principles that sustained it for centuries. Since these principles are poorly understood within the framework of modern medicine, they have been largely discarded. However, older practices are compatible with our current scientifically based approaches and should be re-incorporated into medicine. We should not replace our recent successful approaches. Rather, the older techniques and approaches should be synthesized with our present practices. With such a synthesis, better health should ensue. Without such a synthesis, medicine will become further removed from what you need. Medicine, as it is now evolving, is increasing its potential to do harm. I am concerned that commercial interests, motivated by financial gain, will increasingly exploit your unmet needs for financial gain and that further ill health and dissatisfaction will result.

In the past, when people were considered as integrated, whole individuals, a dimension of good health was afforded. As these traditional approaches were replaced by the "new, scientific" therapies, health care frequently suffered.

You should not be compartmentalized into organ systems, scientific disciplines or medical specialties. Such compartmentalization and specialization have been convenient both for the acquisition of knowledge and for an efficient approach to illness. However, the fact that you are an integrated individual has too often been overlooked. Your mind and body should not be viewed as dissociated. Although this separation is compatible with current medical or scientific thinking, the mind and the body are inseparable.

There is much to be gained by combining the old

with the new. This integrated approach to health care is simply the practice of good medicine. However, since the introduction of any concept requires identification, the term "Behavioral Medicine" will be used to designate what I shall present. These tenets can be taught to doctors and medical students without a radical departure from existing medical standards. Since good health is both the responsibility of the physician and of the patient working together, you must also be made aware of these concepts.

The vicious cycle of the pursuit of health leading to ill health can be broken through the adoption of the principles of Behavioral Medicine. Realistic expectations about your health can be gained. Moreover, recognition of the commercial exploitation of health needs should enhance a sense of reliance upon your own innate resources and decrease dependence upon medications. By weighing the potential risks of health practices against their potential benefits, you will be better able to approach health problems. Your understanding of the principles of Behavioral Medicine will lead to a new perspective of the practice of medicine. Through use of this perspective, you may achieve a better understanding of what constitutes good health and a way to attain it.

2

YOUR MIND AND BODY

IF YOU WERE TOLD that your mind and body did not interact, you might hesitate to accept such a statement. You might remember episodes of fear or anxiety which were accompanied by bodily symptoms of nausea, sweating, weakness or palpitations. Unfortunately, we have come to believe that the mind and the body should be approached separately. Illnesses of the mind are the concern of psychiatrists and psychologists who frequently employ therapeutic verbal techniques, as well as medications. Illnesses of the body are treated by physicians who employ drugs and operative techniques which are directed toward alleviation or cure. Since our bodies are composed of various organ systems, medical and surgical specialists treat our bodily diseases accordingly. "Mind doctors" and "body doctors" regrettably do not always consider us as whole beings. An attempt is now being made to bridge the traditionally separated disciplines of psychiatry and medicine. Behavioral Medicine represents an interdisciplinary approach to health care which incorporates the principles of medicine, physiology, psychiatry and psychology. It enables you as a patient to be viewed as an entire individual. Behavioral Medicine recognizes that your behavior is related to your health and to your illnesses.

Your body is a highly complex entity composed of a number of different, yet coordinated, biological systems. These systems permit effective interaction between our internal and external surroundings. The digestive system functions to process necessary foodstuffs for the body and to eliminate wastes. The acquisition of oxygen, necessary to convert the foodstuffs into energy, is performed by the respiratory system. This system also helps to eliminate carbon dioxide and water, the unused products of energy conversion. The renal, or kidney, system participates in the removal of waste products. The circulatory system distributes blood continuously through approximately 50,000 miles of arteries, capillaries and veins to supply each of our trillions of cells with sufficient fuel to carry out its functions. This system then carries modified and unused fuel to other sites for utilization or elimination. The blood itself, containing red and white cells, constitutes a separate system. The red blood cells bind, transport and release oxygen and carbon dioxide; the white blood cells combat infections and are an integral part of the immunological system of the body. Movement and locomotion are produced by the muscular-skeletal system. The endocrine system regulates the internal environment of our bodies through the secretion of hormones such as insulin, thyroxin and epinephrine (adrenaline). The reproductive system enables the perpetuation of other human beings through elaborate biological and behavioral processes.

These highly differentiated systems are integrated by the nervous system. It is divided anatomically into the central and peripheral nervous systems. The central nervous system is composed of the brain and spinal cord [see Figure 1]. The peripheral nervous system consists of a network of nerves connecting the various internal organs and systems of the body to the central nervous system [see Figure 2]. The central nervous system enables thought and memory to occur. The entire nervous system permits our bodies to interpret consciously and unconsciously our external and internal environments. Nerve endings which are specialized for sight, smell, hearing, taste and the sensations of touch, temperature, pressure and pain supply information. The entire nervous system regulates bodily events such as the circulation of blood, the digestion of food and breathing. The nervous system coordinates bodily responses to the environment. These responses are usually combinations of reactions, some of which reach consciousness and others which do not. When we interpret a situation as dangerous enough to neces-

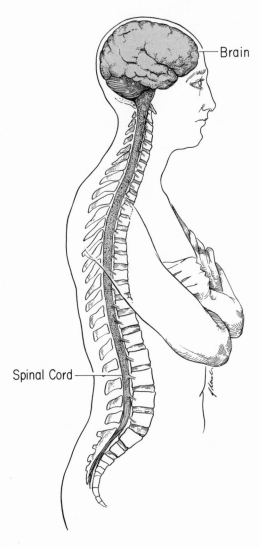

Brain

Spinal Cord

FIGURE 1   THE CENTRAL NERVOUS SYSTEM.

The central nervous system is composed of the brain and the spinal cord.

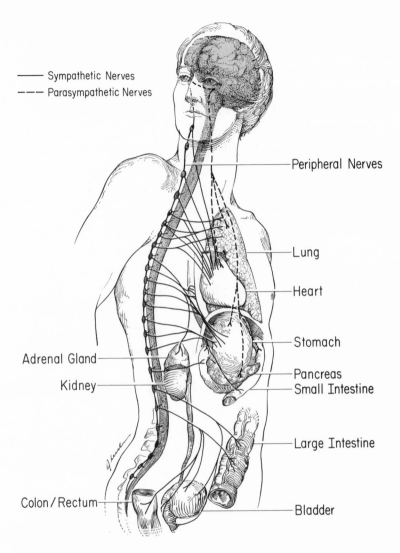

Sympathetic Nerves
Parasympathetic Nerves

Peripheral Nerves

Lung

Heart

Stomach

Adrenal Gland

Pancreas
Small Intestine

Kidney

Large Intestine

Colon / Rectum

Bladder

FIGURE 2   THE CENTRAL NERVOUS SYSTEM
AND THE PERIPHERAL NERVOUS SYSTEM.

The peripheral nervous system is composed of a network of
nerves which connects the various organs and other systems
of the body to the central nervous system.

sitate bodily escape, we are aware of fright and of our running, but we are unaware of the physiological responses of increased metabolism, elevated blood pressure, greater blood flow to the muscles and decreased blood flow to the digestive organs. All our bodily systems are intricately interwoven for optimal function. So how can there be a workable separation of mind and body and how did such an artificial separation come about?

Since the time of Plato, most scholars have believed that the mind and the body were of a different nature. The mind could influence the body and was dominant over the body. The seventeenth-century mathematician and philosopher, René Descartes, assigned a much more important role to the body than did others before him. The mind was no longer the master of the two. In giving the body equal influence, the mind and the body were more easily conceived of as being separate. The modern separation of the mind and the body is clearly traced to Descartes. He emphasized that the body was a machine "so built up and composed of nerves, muscles, veins, blood and skin, that though there were no mind in it at all, it would not cease to have the same [functions]..." Interaction between the mind and the body occurred during such actions as bodily muscular movements "which are due to the direction of the will..." However, what had previously been considered functions of the mind—locomotion and reproduction, for example—were now functions of the body. The mind could will the body to move, to flee from that which is harmful and seek that which is wanted, but action was carried out by the mechanistic muscles and nerves of the body. The mind was responsible for thought and consciousness, which included will, conception of ideas, feelings, understanding, and what Descartes referred to as "the passions" (desire, love, hatred, hope). Descartes considered the mind to be indivisible and nonmaterial and the body to be divisible and material. The mind was subject to reason and God; the body to mechanical laws. The two were separate, each responsible for its own functions, yet interacting in a purely machine-like fashion. Although Descartes's arguments for separation of the mind from the body appear somewhat dated, no one since has completely succeeded in rejecting the concept that the mind and the body are quite distinct.

Attempts have been made to eliminate this distinction by the formation of disciplines such as Psychosomatic Medicine. The concepts of Psychosomatic Medicine provide a theoretical framework which relate mind and body. One of the major teachings is that certain patterns of thought may lead to specific illnesses. For example, repeatedly unexpressed feelings of anger and hostility may be translated into disorders such as high blood pressure or irregular heartbeats. However, because Psychosomatic Medicine has not yet offered definitive therapies for such disorders, it has not substantially altered the belief that the mind and the body are separate.

However, the close interrelation between your mind and body cannot be ignored when modern scientific knowledge is considered. The potential exists for thought processes to lead both to disease and to good health. For instance, can psychological events, events of your mind, lead to death? The concept of "voodoo death" is the extreme example of the potential negative effects of the mind on the body.

VOODOO

Voodoo is a set of religious practices thought to have originated in Africa as a form of ancestor worship. It has often been referred to as black magic or sorcery and is characterized by appeasing rites to the gods. Persons practicing voodoo frequently rely upon trances as a way of communicating with the gods. These deities generally are thought of as individual disembodied spirits which exercise either helpful or harmful influences. Voodoo is practiced chiefly among the native populations of Africa, Haiti, South America and the West Indies, while a similar set of beliefs is found in Australia, New Zealand and various Pacific islands.

Among Australian aboriginal tribes, witch doctors practiced the custom of "pointing the bone," whereby a magic spell was cast into the spirit of the victim. The purpose of such spells was to disturb the spirit of the victim to the extent that disease and death would ensue. Many accounts of death attributed to voodoo have been documented. In 1925 Dr. Herbert Basedow described one such occurrence:

> The man who discovers that he is being boned by an enemy is, indeed, a pitiable sight. He stands aghast, with his eyes staring at the treacherous pointer, and with his hands lifted as though to ward off the lethal medium, which he imagines is pouring into his body. His cheeks blanch and his eyes become glassy, and the expression of his face becomes horribly distorted ... He attempts to shriek but usually the sound chokes in his throat, and all that one might see is froth at his mouth. His body begins to tremble and the muscles twist involuntarily. He sways backwards and falls to the ground, and after a short time appears to be in a swoon; but soon after he writhes as if in mortal agony, and, covering his face with his hands, begins to moan ... His death is only a matter of a comparatively short time.

Many instances of such death, characterized by specific physiological changes, resulted from bone pointing and similar practices. *The success of such practices is dependent upon both the victim's awareness of the spell cast and the victim's strong adherence to his society's belief systems.* These factors lead to the conviction that any hope of escape is impossible. Dr. Walter B. Cannon, a famous Harvard Medical School physiologist who lived at the turn of the twentieth century, discussed this power of the *tapu* (taboo) among the Maori aborigines of New Zealand. The superstitious beliefs associated with their sacred chiefs constituted a powerful, although purely imaginary, barrier. Further, "transgression of that barrier entails the death of the transgressor whenever he becomes aware of what he has done. It is a fatal power of the imagination working through unmitigated terror." Cannon related the incident of a young aborigine who, during a journey, slept at an older friend's home. For breakfast, the friend had prepared a meal consisting of wild hen, a food which the immature were strictly prohibited from eating. The young man demanded to know whether the meal consisted of wild hen and the host responded "No." The young man then ate the meal and departed. Several years later, when the two friends met again, the older man asked his friend whether he would now eat a wild hen. The young man said he would not since he had been solemnly ordered not to do so. The older man laughed and told him how he had been previously tricked into eating this forbidden food. The young man became extremely frightened and started to tremble. Within twenty-four hours, he had died.

Cannon asserted that voodoo death is a very real phenomenon, which can be attributed to a shocking emotional stress, leading to open or repressed terror. He observed that this phenomenon typically occurred among human beings who were so superstitious that they were "bewildered strangers in a hostile world." The social environment is of profound importance in sustaining group morale in a poorly understood world. An individual deprived of this community support is subject to unimaginable terror. As Cannon continued:

> In his isolation the malicious spirits which he believes are all about him and capable of irresistibly and calamitously maltreating him, exert supremely their evil power. Amid this mysterious murk of grim and ominous fatality what has been called "the greatest known extremity of fear," that of an immediate threat of death, fills the terrified victim with powerless misery.

MODERN EQUIVALENTS TO VOODOO DEATH

In the Western world, equivalents to voodoo death have been documented in case histories. Systematic laboratory investigations of death in man resulting from emotional factors cannot be conducted for obvious reasons. However, the case histories provide a basis for analysis of the psychological states which are frequently associated with deaths precipitated by emotional factors. One of these psychological states is characterized by a sense of being powerless and without hope. Dr. George L. Engel, Professor of Psychiatry and Medicine at the University of Rochester Medical Center, believes that the features of helplessness and hopelessness are the essential components of what he has termed the "giving-up–given-up complex."

Engel compiled one hundred newspaper items

from all over the world which focused upon the occurrence of sudden deaths under unusual circumstances. A subsequent analysis of the psychological aspects of the various life situations indicated that the important feature was how the individual responded, not the specific external event or set of circumstances. The overriding feature is a sense of being powerless to cope with changes in the environment.

The following case reports reveal the striking features of so many sudden deaths: the sense of hopelessness and doom preceding the demise. Dr. Leon J. Saul of Media, Pennsylvania, discussed the case history of a 45-year-old professional man. The man found himself in an intolerable situation which necessitated a move to another town. Immediately prior to his move, however, difficulties developed which he felt rendered the move impossible. In a state of anguish, he followed through with his departure plans. He could accept neither his former life situation nor the present one. Yet he could see no other alternative. Approximately half-way to his new location, his train stopped at another town. The man got out to pace on the platform. When the conductor called "All aboard!" the man was convinced he could travel no further; he also felt he could not return. There appeared to be no resolution to his dilemma. He died suddenly of no apparent cause. Previously, there had been no significant medical problems. This case history represents an intolerable life situation, a situation of impasse or no escape. Death probably occurred first on a psychological level in a situation of perceived utter hopelessness.

Saul also reported the case of a 33-year-old woman who was married and had four children. Her medical history was unremarkable, although she occasionally experienced mild asthma. Her marriage was troubled, as her husband possessed a violent temper and had struck her on occasion. Several times, while in a rage, he smashed furniture. She was afraid of him and complained about his behavior. Although he substantially modified his attitudes and improved his behavior, she became increasingly unhappy. The woman developed paranoid delusions, claiming that her husband was plotting against her and the children. She severed ties with her parents. Attempts at treatment were unsuccessful. She felt that she could no longer live with her husband because of her fear of his plots. However, she felt that she could not leave him. The situation represented one of no escape. At this time she developed difficulty in her breathing and died unexpectedly, despite prompt medical attention in a fine hospital.

The last case presented by Saul is that of a 40-year-old man who came from a family of prominence and wealth. The man did not lack material goods but he lacked the capacity for independence and responsibility. His parents obtained important positions for him, hoping that responsibility would mature him. Although he enjoyed the income and the prestige that these positions conferred, he ignored the job requirements. His wife left him and he was soon unemployed. He could not find another job and he craved the money and success that he had had in order to maintain his self-esteem. Moreover, at this time his family suffered financial losses. The man's plight worsened when he contracted gambling debts and his family steadfastly refused to help him. In fear of being physically beaten if he failed to pay his debts, and receiving no support from his parents, the man saw no avenue of escape. Immediately after phoning his mother from his desk and receiving an adamant "No" to his request for money, the man died suddenly.

Yet another case history of a sudden death, characterized by a pervading sense of hopelessness and helplessness, was reported by Dr. John C. Coolidge of Cambridge, Massachusetts. He described the circumstances of a middle-aged woman who was undergoing psychoanalysis. She had expressed feelings of uselessness and was convinced that death was the only solution to an intolerable situation. She felt trapped in an unhappy marriage but seemed unable to escape it. She was acutely sensitive to rejection. After suffering a series of rejections by her husband, her only child and her psychoanalyst, she collapsed very unexpectedly. Her heart stopped completely, after a period of beating in a dangerous, irregular fashion (ventricular fibrillation). Autopsy findings later gave no indication of any heart disease. Coolidge felt that understanding of the patient's psychodynamics clarified the situation. As a child, the patient had been severely disciplined to restrict all spontaneous behavior and emotional expression. The patient's past history of physiological repercussions during times of stress led the author to conclude that "the only route physiologically available for discharge of emotional tensions was internal and somatic."

The impact of a state of hopelessness upon well-being is also evident in a case discussed by Dr. James L. Mathis, of the University of Oklahoma Medical Center, in an article entitled "A Sophisticated Version of Voodoo Death." A 53-year-old, previously healthy, married male succumbed over a nine-month period to a series of asthma attacks which were directly traceable to his mother's influence. Medical management on each occasion resulted in improvement, but the patient became increasingly depressed and expressed feelings of hopelessness. The man wished to complete a business transaction that went against his mother's wishes, and his mother had predicted that "dire results" would ensue if he did not follow her advice. Repeated reminders of this prediction and her warning that "something will strike you" following the completion of the business transaction culminated in a number of asthma attacks and convulsions, and required numerous hospitalizations. Psychiatric consultation was sought to alleviate the man's depression, which was characterized by repeated claims that his condition was hopeless. His death several months later was immediately preceded by a telephone call to his mother during which he announced his plans for re-investing his money in another business. He told her that he would not need her assistance. His mother terminated the conversation with her familiar prediction of "dire results." The man was found dead an hour later. Mathis notes that the history of this man's illness is remarkably consistent with descriptions of voodoo death. Psychological death induced by the "malevolent wish of a thwarted mother" represents the modern-day counterpart to death resulting from the incantations of a primitive witch doctor.

Extreme fright is another psychological state associated with sudden death. Two early accounts are found in the New Testament, Book of Acts, chapter 5:

> But a man named Ananias with his wife Sapphira sold a piece of property, and with his wife's knowledge he kept back some of the proceeds, and brought only a part and laid it at the apostle's feet. But Peter said, "Ananias, why has Satan filled your heart to lie to the Holy Spirit and to keep back part of the proceeds of the land? While it remained unsold, did it not remain your own? And after it was sold, was it not at your disposal? How is it that you have contrived this deed in your heart? You have not lied to men but to God." When Ananias heard these words, he fell down and died. . . .
>
> After an interval of about three hours his wife came in, not knowing what had happened. And Peter said to her, "Tell me whether you sold the

land for so much." And she said, "Yes, for so much." But Peter said to her, "How is it that you have agreed together to tempt the Spirit of the Lord? Hark, the feet of those that have buried your husband are at the door, and they will carry you out." Immediately she fell down at his feet and died.

In 1860 a sudden death due to fear was reported in the *British Medical Journal*. A seemingly healthy housemaid was caught stealing food, and she immediately dropped dead. Autopsy did not reveal any notable pathological changes.

Dr. J. C. Barker of Shrewsbury, Shropshire, England described a man in his early 40s who was admitted to the hospital in a very agitated condition and was excessively overbreathing. There was no previous medical history of significance. On the ward he desperately clutched at the medical personnel, crying repeatedly, "Doctor, doctor, I am going to die. I am going to die, please don't let me die, please don't let me die, please, please..." He was given oxygen and a pharmacological agent to ease his breathing. He cried out again, then abruptly slumped down in the bed. Within a half hour after being admitted, he was dead. A thorough autopsy revealed no evidence of significant pathology. It was concluded that the man had "died of fright."

Dr. Erich Menninger von Lerchenthal, a Viennese physician, discussed several instances of sudden death due to fright. One of the cases he cited was taken from the diary of Joseph Hayden, who allegedly wrote on April 25, 1792:

On the 26th of March at the concert of Mr. Bartholemon (London) there was an English clergyman who while hearing my Andante sank into the deepest melancholy because of the fact that on the previous night he had dreamed of such an Andante which announced his death. He immediately left the company, went to bed and today I heard through Mr. Bartholemon that this clergyman had died.

Menninger von Lerchenthal also reported the gruesome case of an assistant who was widely disliked by the students at a college. He was condemned to a mock death ceremony in a serious fashion. The assistant was held down so that his head lay on a chopping block, and his eyes were covered with a bandage. One student simulated the sound of a swinging axe and another student then dropped a wet, warm cloth on the assistant's neck. The assistant died immediately.

The relative frequency of death due to fright and other intense emotions is afforded by analysis of sudden deaths of soldiers subjected to the stress of World War II. A comprehensive investigation of over 40,000 autopsy protocols received by the Army Institute of Pathology was undertaken in 1946 by Dr. Alan R. Moritz and Dr. Norman Zamcheck. While many of the reported sudden deaths, numbering approximately 1000, could later be attributed to specific causes, cardiovascular diseases in particular, there still remained at least 140 carefully investigated cases characterized by essentially normal postmortem findings. Thorough pathological examinations were frequently supplemented by toxicological studies, that is, chemical tests for poisons. The postmortem findings were not adequate to explain the unexpected failure of circulation, respiration or other immediate cause of death. Therefore, the number of deaths due to fright constituted, at most, 14 percent of sudden deaths in this investigation.

PROBABLE PHYSIOLOGICAL
MECHANISM OF VOODOO DEATH

The probable physiological mechanism of sudden death is a disruption of normal heart functioning. Death which occurs *suddenly or unexpectedly, within a period of several minutes, in a person with apparently good or stable health,* is almost invariably due to cessation of the circulation of blood. Such sudden death is due to malfunctioning of the circulatory system. Death which is due to alterations of normal function in other organ systems usually is preceded by ill health and occurs much more slowly. Therefore, the sudden deaths related to very intense psychological states such as hopelessness-helplessness, overwhelming fear and other extreme emotions are almost certainly related to circulatory events. To better understand the mechanism of these deaths, a more detailed description of the circulatory system is necessary.

The circulatory system distributes vital fuels to all

functional units of the body. These fuels, such as foodstuffs and oxygen, are essential for the production of energy, which is necessary for the efficient functioning of the different bodily systems. The blood carries these fuels in the blood vessels: the arteries, veins and capillaries. The heart is the pump. The pumping action of the heart is achieved by the contraction of the heart muscle, which squeezes the blood from the heart into various blood vessels. The heart is filled with blood from other blood vessels when it relaxes between the contractions. One heartbeat consists of a contraction phase and a relaxation phase. A continuous flow of blood is maintained by the alternating contraction and relaxation of the pumping heart. The control of both the rate and rhythm of this mechanical pumping action of the heart is electrical. There is a close coupling of the mechanical events with the electrical events.

The heart has a natural electrical capacity which leads to periodic electrical discharges. These electrical discharges stimulate the muscular cells of the heart to contract in an exquisitely coordinated fashion, to produce effective pumping. These discharges occur regularly in a healthy heart, between sixty and one hundred times a minute. The *electrical* activity of the heart is measured by an electrocardiogram. The electrocardiogram records the sum of the electrical forces generated by the heart. Small metal plates placed on the skin detect these electrical forces, which are transmitted throughout the body.

The electrical impulses are then conducted along wires from the metal plates to the electrocardiograph. The impulses are modified within the electrocardiograph so that they may be recorded on standardized paper [see Figure 3]. The electrocardiogram is not a measure of the mechanical pumping action of the heart, but rather indicates the rhythm of the heartbeat and the electrical integrity of the heart. However, the components of the electrocardiogram can be related to specific mechanical events [see Figure 4].

The electrical rhythm of the heart is not only determined by control centers in the heart, which regulate the electrical discharges, but is also influenced by nerve impulses originating in the brain. These impulses are transmitted to the heart by sympathetic nerves and parasympathetic nerves [see Figure 5]. An increase in the number of impulses along the sympathetic nerves to the heart results in an increased heart rate [see Figure 6]. An increase in the number of impulses along the parasympathetic nerves to the heart, usually carried along the vagus nerve, results in a decreased heart rate [see Figure 7]. The heart rate is determined primarily by the energy needs of the body. During exercise, more energy is required by the cells and organs of the body and heart rate increases. During rest, the energy requirements of the body are lower and heart rate decreases. There are continual adjustments made in response to bodily requirements. For example, if there is a decrease in blood pressure, that is, the force with which

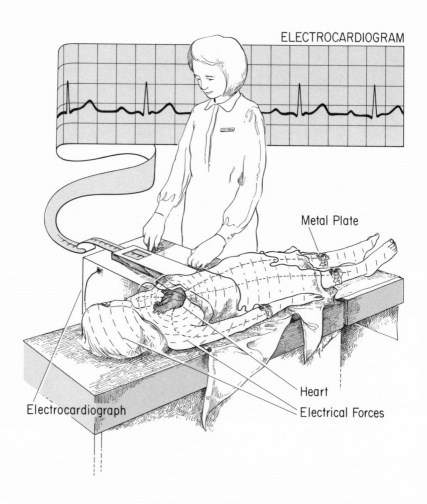

Metal Plate

Electrocardiograph

Heart

Electrical Forces

FIGURE 3   AN ELECTROCARDIOGRAM BEING RECORDED.

Small metal plates, which are placed on the skin, detect the electrical forces generated by the heart. Wires conduct these impulses to the electrocardiograph. Within the electrocardiograph, the impulses are modified to a graphic form. The impulses are then recorded on electrocardiographic paper. This recording is an electrocardiogram. The electrocardiogram in the diagram is normal. An enlarged electrocardiogram is portrayed behind the technician.

36

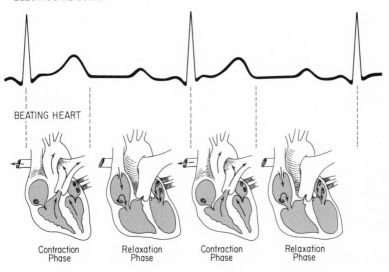

ELECTROCARDIOGRAM

BEATING HEART

Contraction Phase   Relaxation Phase   Contraction Phase   Relaxation Phase

FIGURE 4   THE RELATION OF THE ELECTROCARDIOGRAM
TO SPECIFIC MECHANICAL PUMPING
ACTIONS OF THE HEART.

The electrical and mechanical events of the heartbeat are
closely coordinated. During specific electrical events, recorded on the electrocardiogram, there is mechanical contraction. This contraction is regularly followed by mechanical
relaxation of the heart which is associated with other specific
electrical events. During the "contraction phase" of the
heartbeat, blood is pumped from the heart into the large
arteries. During the "relaxation phase," the heart is filled
with blood from the large veins. The heart rate diagrammed
in this figure is 75 beats per minute.

37

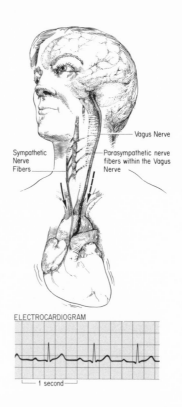

Vagus Nerve

Sympathetic
Nerve
Fibers

Parasympathetic nerve
fibers within the Vagus
Nerve

ELECTROCARDIOGRAM

1 second

FIGURE 5 THE ACTION OF THE SYMPATHETIC AND
PARASYMPATHETIC NERVOUS SYSTEMS
UPON THE HEART.

The sympathetic and parasympathetic nerve fibers are part
of the peripheral nervous system. Some of these sympathetic
and parasympathetic nerves are connected to the heart. Most
of the parasympathetic nerves are carried by one common
nerve, the vagus nerve. The impulses along the sympathetic
nerves are represented by solid arrows. The impulses along
the parasympathetic nerves are represented by broken arrows. In this diagram, there is a balance of impulses travel-
ing along the sympathetic and parasympathetic nerves and
the heart rate is within normal limits. Normal limits of heart
rate are usually considered to be between 60 and 100 beats
per minute. The heart rate in the diagram is 75 beats per
minute.

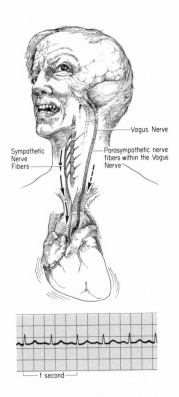

Vagus Nerve

Sympathetic
Nerve
Fibers

Parasympathetic nerve
fibers within the Vagus
Nerve

1 second

FIGURE 6 THE ACTION OF THE SYMPATHETIC NERVES
UPON THE HEART.

In this diagram there are increased impulses along the sympathetic nerves to the heart, indicated by the solid arrows. The heart rate is increased to 125 beats per minute. Although the heart rate is rapid, the other aspects of the electrocardiogram are normal.

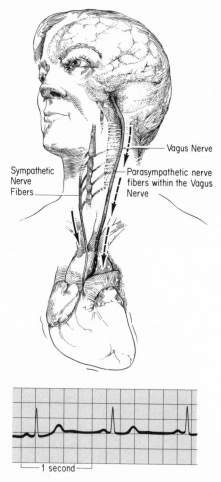

Vagus Nerve

Sympathetic Nerve Fibers

Parasympathetic nerve fibers within the Vagus Nerve

1 second

FIGURE 7 THE ACTION OF THE PARASYMPATHETIC NERVES UPON THE HEART.

There are increased impulses along the parasympathetic nerves to the heart in this diagram. The impulses are indicated by the broken arrows. These impulses travel along the vagus nerve. The heart rate in this diagram is slowed to 58 beats per minute. Although the heart rate is relatively slow, the other components of the electrocardiogram are normal.

blood is pumped, heart rate will increase to compensate for the lower pressure. If blood pressure increases, heart rate decreases.

All our organs require a continuous fresh supply of blood. The heart must therefore pump steadily without interruption, to maintain this blood flow and to maintain life. The proper functioning of electrical and mechanical activities of the heart, as well as their integrated coupling, insures adequate pumping. When either the electrical performance, the mechanical performance or some combination of the two is impaired, blood flow is altered. The various organs have different degrees of tolerance to impaired blood flow. The brain is the most sensitive organ. It cannot tolerate an interruption of blood flow for more than five or six *seconds*. If the brain fails to receive fresh blood for longer than this time, unconsciousness and fainting result. Fainting may be viewed as performing the physiological function of increasing blood flow to the brain because after a faint, an individual is usually lying flat. Blood then flows more easily to the brain, since it does not have to overcome the force of gravity necessitated by the normal upright posture.* If the blood flow to the brain remains inadequate, permanent brain damage results. Soon thereafter, other organs undergo permanent damage. The degree of damage is usually determined by the

---

* After a person faints, it is therefore inadvisable to have that individual sit or stand immediately. The posture of lying down is very important for increasing blood flow to the brain. In fact, to increase blood flow to the brain further, the person's legs are sometimes lifted.

duration of interrupted blood flow. Bodily functions may become so impeded that death occurs.

The electrical component of the heartbeat can be markedly affected by emotions. When you become emotionally upset your heart rate increases due to increased stimulation of the sympathetic nerves. Fainting, which is frequently associated with fright or emotional distress such as the sight of blood, is often due to unbalanced responses of the sympathetic and parasympathetic nervous systems. Immediately prior to fainting, there is a sudden decrease in blood pressure and an *inappropriate* slowing of the heart rate. The normal compensatory mechanism which produces increased blood pressure by increasing the heart rate does not occur. Blood flow to the brain is interrupted and fainting results. Then, since the person is lying down, blood flow to the brain *almost invariably* increases within several seconds and the person rapidly regains consciousness. Although fainting may result in injury from the fall itself, it is usually not a serious or dangerous occurrence if it is not a frequent event.

However, when fainting is caused by a sudden dangerous irregularity of the heartbeat, adequate blood flow cannot occur even when the person is lying down and permanent damage or death often occurs. The extreme emotional disturbances which have previously been described in the cases of sudden death probably caused a dangerous irregularity of the electrical component of the heartbeat. The subse-

quent inadequate blood flow would account for many
of these sudden deaths.

ANIMAL EXPERIMENTS AND
SUDDEN DEATH

Data from animal experiments support the conclu-
sions drawn from the numerous case histories. Animal
experiments have simulated the condition of hopelessness-helplessness. Death ensued due to an abnormal heart rhythm, that is, an electrical abnormality
of the heart. Dr. Curt P. Richter of Johns Hopkins
University experimentally induced sudden death in
rats. He first measured the duration of survival in
domesticated rats after they were placed in specially
designed, water-filled glass cylinders. A small number of rats died within five to ten minutes after immersion, while others, which were genetically similar,
swam as long as eighty-one hours before succumbing.
He then conducted the same experiment using wild
rats and found that all these "fierce, aggressive, and
suspicious" animals died within one to fifteen minutes
after immersion. Subsequent investigations established that the deaths of the wild rats were closely
related to factors which eliminated any hope of escape and were not attributable to exhaustion. Being
held firmly in the experimenter's hand, thereby pre-
venting biting and escaping, as well as being con-
fined in the water-filled glass cylinder, were the two
most important situations which contributed to rapid

demise. The combination of these two situations further hastened the onset of death. Richter could forestall sudden death by holding the wild rats for very brief periods of time and then freeing them. He could also forestall death by repeatedly immersing them in water for several minutes at a time before rescuing them. He reasoned that the rats quickly learned the situation was not actually hopeless. Thereafter these rats resumed their aggressive behavior, tried to escape and showed no signs of giving up. Wild rats conditioned in this manner swam as long or longer than did the domesticated rats.

Recent investigations using laboratory rats have further established the importance of psychological and environmental factors implicated in sudden death. Drs. Robert A. Rosellini, Yitzchak M. Binik and Martin E. P. Seligman of the University of Pennsylvania also placed rats in a swimming situation which lasted a maximum of one hour. Domesticated rats which had been reared in isolation from other rats often died suddenly when placed in a swimming environment. Rats which were reared with three or four other rats in the same cage did not die as frequently when placed in the stressful swimming environment. Moreover, handling of the animals raised communally did not significantly increase the percentage of animals dying. Handling of the animals which were reared in isolation increased the percentage of sudden deaths. The vulnerability to sudden death was influenced by the previous experience of being reared alone or communally.

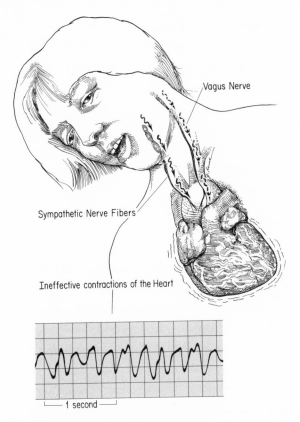

Vagus Nerve

Sympathetic Nerve Fibers

Ineffective contractions of the Heart

└─ 1 second ─┘

FIGURE 8   VENTRICULAR FIBRILLATION.

There is a marked imbalance and disruption of the normal impulses along the nerve fibers of the sympathetic and parasympathetic nervous system. The normal rhythmic electrical activities of the heart have become chaotic. The electrocardiogram in the diagram is strikingly abnormal. It is indicative of the life-threatening disturbance, ventricular fibrillation. The normal contraction and relaxation phases of the heartbeat are no longer present. The heart quivers ineffectively, its surface appearing like a can of live worms. No effective blood flow is present since the heart cannot be filled with blood and the heart cannot expel blood. The organs are deprived of a fresh supply of blood. Death will rapidly ensue if a normal heartbeat does not return.

45

The mode of death in rats forced to swim has been documented by Richter. He constructed electrodes which were attached to the rats prior to immersion so that an electrocardiogram could be obtained while the rats were swimming. There was first a marked slowing of the heart rate, followed by stoppage of the electrical activity of the heart. This stoppage led to interruption of mechanical pumping and resulted in rapid death.

The sudden deaths induced in animals are analogous to voodoo death. Voodoo death is probably a cardiac death related to an electrical disturbance of the heartbeat. The specific abnormal rhythms of the heart include *extremely rapid* heartbeating (ventricular fibrillation or ventricular tachycardia) or *extremely slow* heartbeating or complete stoppage of the heartbeat. Extremely rapid heartbeating, several hundred or more beats per minute, is associated with ineffective pumping. There is insufficient time for the heart to fill with blood in the relaxation phase of the heartbeat [see Figure 8]. The pump is not primed. Extremely slow beating is also associated with decreased pumping. These abnormal heart rates are mediated through an imbalance of the sympathetic and parasympathetic nervous systems. These systems are, in turn, markedly influenced by areas of the brain which are related to emotions and thought processes.

DISEASE STATES AND
PSYCHOLOGICAL FACTORS

Death related to emotions is not very common. The numerous case histories which have been cited constitute a major portion of the available literature concerning this subject. However, since death has been shown to be related to psychological factors, it is quite reasonable to expect that certain disease states may be brought about by such factors. The circulatory system again affords examples. Most irregularities of the heartbeat are *not* associated with death. Even some of the very serious irregularities, ventricular tachycardia and ventricular fibrillation, can be tolerated if they are not prolonged.

There is a growing body of evidence which associates the onset of many of these episodes of markedly altered heart rhythm with emotional events. Modern technology has made possible the monitoring and recording of every heartbeat. Such monitoring is routinely done in coronary care units of hospitals. Analysis of the results of this monitoring, in conjunction with the results of other evaluations, has yielded insights into the relation of psychological events and irregularities of the heartbeat. One excellent example of such analysis is the detailed and thorough report of Drs. Bernard Lown, John V. Temte, Peter Reich, Charles Gaughan, Quentin Regestein and Hamid Hai of Harvard University. They described the close association of life-threatening disorders of heart rhythm to psychological factors in a 39-year-old educator. The patient was a healthy athletic man with no previous serious illnesses. One day, after "rough-housing" with his two teenaged daughters, he suddenly collapsed. He turned a bluish (cyanotic) color and developed an extremely labored pattern of breathing often seen immediately prior to death. He also developed seizure-like movements. Fortunately, his wife was a Registered Nurse and she immediately started cardiopulmonary resuscitation, which revived the patient. When he reached the hospital, his cardiac rhythm was noted to be ventricular fibrillation. His irregular heart rhythm was converted to a more normal rhythm by a medical team using the modern therapeutic techniques. Subsequent evaluations established that his heart was structurally and functionally healthy; there was no underlying heart disease. However, continuous electrocardiographic monitoring revealed that several different types of abnormal heart rhythms were frequently present, including bursts of ventricular tachycardia.

The investigators tested the efficacy of various drugs and also performed psychiatric evaluations. During the psychiatric evaluations, the patient was judged to be hyperalert and defensive. He was very competitive and had acquired his higher education despite many difficulties. He often felt very angry and dealt with his anger by vigorously exercising, which he did alone. The content of his dreams was frequently violent. The psychiatric evaluations indicated that the control of his aggression represented a major aspect of his life. Six months prior to the patient's illness, he had had his first career setback. His wife was not supportive of his psychological needs since her father had recently died and she was depressed. His teenaged daughters were spending increasing time away from home.

The psychiatrists also suggested that the patient had very strong sexual restraints. The rough-housing with his daughters, which immediately preceded his collapse, provoked both erotic and aggressive impulses in him. The girls were sexually mature, and during this episode of play the patient felt that there was much sexual provocation. The play was interrupted by the sound of the doorbell. When one daughter went to the door, he slumped to the floor; his last words before unconsciousness were: "I'm sorry."

The patient's heart rhythm was continuously monitored before, during and after the psychiatric interviews. Even though he had been free of ventricular tachycardia for an entire week, this irregularity was recorded immediately after a psychiatrist entered the room. The frequency of other less serious heart rhythms, ventricular premature beats, also increased dramatically during the psychiatric interviews. The underlying mechanism for these irregular heartbeats was felt to be excessive stimulation of the sympathetic nervous system due to this patient's angry, competitive and aggressive impulses [see Figure 6].

(At last report, nine months after hospital discharge, this patient was doing well on a combined medical, psychiatric and behavioral regimen. Twenty-four-hour monitoring of his heartbeat revealed no abnormalities. He was taking medications, jogging several miles a day and meditating regularly. Further, he had been encouraged to verbalize his violent dreams.)

Excessive stimulation of the parasympathetic nervous system may also result from emotional events. Adams-Stokes attacks are characterized by sudden episodes of fainting and unconsciousness which are sometimes accompanied by convulsions. The heartbeat stops or becomes extremely slowed for ten seconds or more. Blood flow to the brain and other organs is inadequate and the symptoms appear. If a normal heart rate does not spontaneously return, death occurs. If adequate heartbeating returns rapidly, the patient will awaken. The condition is generally fatal within a few years after clinical onset, since there is an increased probability of a prolonged episode with repeated attacks. Adams-Stokes attacks can usually be ascribed to a definable heart disease. Adams-Stokes attacks differ from "simple" fainting in that simple fainting is not associated with an underlying disorder of the heart and is not associated with death.

In 1961 Dr. Kenneth Meinhardt and Dr. Herbert A. Robinson of Norwalk, California, reported the case history of a 28-year-old male with a diagnosis of Adams-Stokes attacks. Prior to the onset of these Adams-Stokes episodes, the patient had had no cardiac symptoms or other evidence of heart disease. His fainting episodes were produced by excessive parasympathetic nervous system activity, or vagal stimulation, which markedly slowed heart rate [see Figure 7]. His emotional conflicts had the effect of increasing nerve impulses along the vagal nerve. During this patient's Adams-Stokes attacks his heart rate slowed to about forty beats per minute. He was given appropriate medicines that stimulated his heart to beat more rapidly. However, during an emotional outbreak at home, in which the patient angrily accused his wife of neglecting him and the children, he experienced repeated episodes of fainting. These were not controlled by increased medication. Under continued medical management he gradually recovered. He remained well, except when he became emotionally overwrought. One fainting episode occurred when he was visited by his wife's former lover. He also experienced attacks during a series of psychiatric interviews.

These interviews revealed that the patient had intense dependency needs which were not fulfilled. His father had died unexpectedly when the patient was age 6, arousing feelings of guilt and bitterness in the patient. Each mention of his father's death would cause the patient to flush and cry uncontrollably. He experienced a very unhappy family life; he felt that his mother was cold and emotionless and he was unable to relate to his stepfather. He left home at age 15 to live and work in a construction camp. At age 21 he married. This marriage was described by the patient as "stormy." He and his wife were separated after a period of five years, followed by a reunion several months later. Before marriage, he had perceived her as a withdrawn and "mousy type" person. Despite this, he felt that he loved her and thought she would be a good wife and mother. After marriage, he described her as "almost the extreme opposite type, like a streetwalker." Both of them constantly argued at home and the children developed behavior problems. The patient felt that his wife was inadequate. At one point he had been involved in an extramarital relationship, with an older "motherly" married woman, which terminated unhappily.

During these psychiatric interviews the Adams-Stokes episodes followed a predictable sequence of events. He discussed his feelings of being unloved and neglected by both his mother and wife, as well as by his friends and employers. When reflecting upon this topic, he typically became very angry. After his anger dissipated he would become tense and brace his body rigidly. A flush of color would spread across his face, his mouth would quiver and he would then burst into stifled sobs. Once he cried out, "If anyone saw me, I'd die!"

Each Adams-Stokes episode during the interviews took place when his body tensed and as he was attempting to conceal his grief. Psychiatric analysis of the patient indicated that he was generally a very submissive person. Underlying this passive exterior, however, there seemed to be evidence of extreme anger and rage, which the patient was able to control only by exerting supreme effort. Concomitantly, the patient feared that he would not be able to control his rage, and hence, it was reasoned, he developed symptoms which culminated in fainting episodes.

The intense emotions of rage and fear experienced by this patient typically induce increased sympathetic nervous system activity [see Figure 6]. The physiology of Adams-Stokes syndrome in this patient, however, consisted of increased parasympathetic nervous system activity, or an increased vagal response. Meinhardt and Robinson, using tenets of Psychosomatic Medicine, hypothesize that a shift occurred from sympathetic to parasympathetic nerve discharges as a result of inhibition of sympathetic nervous system activity. The patient was susceptible to feelings of rage, yet his dependency needs prohibited him from expressing this anger. The authors hypothesize that the loneliness and grief, also intensely felt by this man, were characterized by a corresponding physiological shift from sympathetic to parasympathetic discharges. When there was a sufficient shift to the vagal response, the patient experienced an Adams-Stokes attack.*

The pioneering work of Drs. Thomas H. Holmes

---

* There is no information concerning the patient's subsequent medical history. In 1961 permanent cardiac pacemakers were not routinely available. Therefore this optimal therapy for excessive vagal nerve activity was not possible. These permanent pacemakers, which are surgically placed under the skin, monitor the heartbeat. When the heartbeat becomes too slow or stops, the pacemaker senses this disruption and is automatically programmed to deliver a periodic electric current to the heart. These electric currents produce a regular heartbeat. When the natural heartbeat

and Richard H. Rahe, initiated at the University of Washington Medical School, supports the concept that stressful psychological events can be implicated in the rapid development of other disease states. In 1967 they reported the results of extensive interviews with 394 individuals of different ages and from various socioeconomic levels. They were able to assign relative risks to specific life events most frequently associated with disease in the subsequent year. The most stressful event was the death of a spouse. Other life-change events which rendered a person susceptible to disease were (in decreasing order of significance) divorce, marital separation, jail term, death of a close family member, personal injury or illness, marriage, being fired at work, marital reconciliation and retirement. Yet other life situations which had an impact upon health were change in health of a family member, pregnancy, sexual difficulties, addition of a family member, business adjustment, change in financial state and death of a close friend.

The findings of Holmes and Rahe should not be interpreted as being invariably predictive of developing a disease rapidly after a stressful life-change event. Your *chances* of developing a disease are simply increased. The major life-change events which increased the likelihood of disease onset are those

---

returns, the pacemaker shuts off. Such a pacemaker may be viewed as an artificial reserve stimulator to maintain a regular heartbeat. They are life-saving devices and represent a remarkable medical-technological achievement. They usually function well, requiring only battery replacement every several years.

usually associated with grief. It is interesting, however, that major life-change events which are considered to be pleasant also had a negative impact upon health.

A strong argument can be made which relates stressful psychological events to diseases which have a slow rate of development. Hypertension, or high blood pressure, is one such disease. Stressful situations are associated with transient elevations of blood pressure; repeated stressful events may even result in permanent high blood pressure.

Little controversy exists within the medical profession concerning the importance of psychological events in making *already existing* diseases worse. Dr. Louis H. Sigler, a New York cardiologist, documented changes in the electrical properties of the heart on electrocardiographic recordings in five patients. The patients had either established heart disease or symptoms highly suggestive of heart disease. Each patient had an electrocardiogram while resting quietly, which served as a basis for comparisons. Then, while the electrocardiographic recording continued, each discussed emotionally disturbing situations. One patient, a remarried 58-year-old woman, considered her new husband cruel. When talking about her disappointments and unhappiness, she developed electrocardiographic abnormalities. A second patient, a 77-year-old man, had established a successful catering business after years of considerable hard work. He later had to sell it at considerable financial loss. When discussing these business problems, he too developed electrocardiographic abnormalities. A very nervous 68-year-old woman developed abnormal changes while expressing concern and anxiety about her very ill sister. Similar electrocardiographic abnormalities were recorded in a 65-year-old man when he was discussing his experiences in a German concentration camp. He had witnessed the deaths of several members of his family and had been frequently threatened with death himself. Yet another case history reported by Sigler was that of a 69-year-old woman who exhibited electrocardiographic changes when she talked about the deaths of three sisters.

Rheumatoid arthritis (a joint disease), ulcerative colitis (a bowel disease) and asthma are other recognized examples of diseases which are aggravated by psychological stress. The course of most diseases may indeed be adversely altered if a person is subjected to excessive stress or is not motivated to get well.

The infectious diseases are caused by identifiable microorganisms, such as bacteria or viruses. Infectious hepatitis, which is caused by a virus, is an excellent example. The venereal diseases, such as syphilis or gonorrhea, are also clearly attributable to microorganisms. However, psychological factors do influence some infectious diseases. Recurrent infections of the virus herpes simplex produce "fever blisters" or "cold sores." Most adults have this virus within them at all times in a quiescent state. The virus often resides around the mouth and nostrils. There is little evidence that this infection of herpes simplex is ever completely eliminated. The herpes simplex infections become manifest when an individual's resistance to disease is lowered by the presence of another illness, such as the common cold, or by a disease causing fever. In some individuals, specific situations, such as exposure to sunlight, cause these herpes simplex sores to appear. However, many observers have reported the frequent appearance of herpes simplex infections after emotional upsets. For example, Dr. Robert Heilig and Dr. Hans Hoff of the University of Vienna were able to bring about the manifestations of these herpes simplex infections in three patients. They reminded the patients, while under hypnosis, of unpleasant situations, for example the deaths of loved ones. Dr. Jerome M. Schneck, while a medical officer at Fort MacArthur, California, described a soldier who could anticipate the sores of his herpes simplex infection appearing soon after experiencing hostile emotions. The soldier could prevent the sores by channeling his feelings into activities such as reading, getting drunk or immersion in hard work. Dr. Harvey Blank and Dr. Morris W. Brody of the University of Pennsylvania and Temple University described nine patients whose recurrent attacks of herpes simplex were unresponsive to routine medical care. However, the recurrent manifestations were effectively terminated after brief psychotherapy. Therefore, if attacks of herpes simplex infections may serve as a model, even diseases directly attributable to specific viruses are related to psychological factors.

However, for some diseases there is virtually no

evidence linking them to emotional events. It is unlikely that various birth defects, for example, those of the heart or those of the bones and joints, have any direct relation to emotional factors. It is equally unlikely that the diseases due to inborn deficits of metabolism, such as diabetes, are related to psychological events.

In this chapter the concept of the mind as separate from the body has been shown to be untenable. The possibility of psychological events exacerbating disease, leading to disease or even leading to death has been discussed. However, as Erich Menninger von Lerchenthal pointed out in 1936: "Although death which psychic efforts have helped to bring about is often clear, one sees the psychic influence on the prolongation of life only if one looks for it." Can an understanding of the mind-body relation be used to prevent disease and contribute to better health? If so, what are the mechanisms involved? The next chapter will discuss how you may achieve better health by rejecting the concept of the mind-body dichotomy.

3

Medical practice had little technology of proven value to offer patients until the latter part of the nineteenth century. Before this time, we had been subjected to "purging, puking, poisoning, puncturing, cutting, cupping, blistering, bleeding, leeching, heating, freezing, sweating, and shocking." Physicians have treated our battle wounds with boiling oil and red-hot pokers, have fed us lizard's blood, crushed spiders, crocodile dung, putrid meat, bear fat, fox lungs, eunuch fat and moss scraped from the skull of a hanged criminal.

Such therapeutic concoctions and procedures were by modern medical standards quite worthless, and sometimes harmful. How is it then that throughout history, the doctor or healer has managed to retain his relatively respected position and achieve success in the treatment of disease? It is apparently due to the profound psychological effect of the physician upon the patient, the confidence he instilled and the solace he provided. From antiquity to this era, the physician himself has been a significant factor in the treatment of the patient. Until recently, this was the physician's most potent tool in restoring his patient to good health. Sometimes it was his only effective therapy.

To better understand the nonspecific elements of medical treatment, whether they are called "involvement," "rapport," "empathy" or "samaritanism," we should consider healing practices throughout the ages, before the advent of scientifically based medicine. In so-called primitive cultures, various magico-religious healers relied extensively upon such nonspecific treatment factors. Although there is much cross-cultural variation, there appears to be substantial similarity between the roles assigned to the various types of healers. In American Indian medicine, the central healer was, and in some places still is, the medicine man, whom ethnologists frequently refer to by the Asian term *shaman*. Sometimes the healing role was assumed by an herbalist. Regardless of the term used, the functions of these healers had basic similarities.

Dr. Jean Martin Charcot, a famous nineteenth-century French neurologist, once stated that "the best inspirer of hope is the best physician." The success of the shaman in many primitive societies has been attributed primarily to psychological factors rather than to the intrinsic value of the therapies themselves. Indeed, the shaman, or medicine man, can be viewed as an early psychotherapist. It has long been recognized that the faith of the patient greatly affects his recovery. The implicit confidence that some American Indians, for example, placed in the shaman has been compared to the trust of a patient in a more technically competent physician. The ceremonies and prayers which constituted an integral part of primitive life enhanced this feeling of trust. Josiah Gregg, a Santa Fe trader, commented in the 1830s upon the staunch faith of the Comanche Indians in their medicine men. Gregg suggested that the repetitious singing rituals, designed to frighten away the evil demons from a diseased person, hastened recovery through their effects upon the imagination. Hence, despite the shaman's reliance upon a variety of medicinal and physical aids, his most powerful tools were psychological, consisting of suggestion, persuasion, illusion, fear and hypnosis. The faith of the people in the shaman and the shaman's faith in himself contributed to his success.

Despite the beneficial psychological effects of shamanistic ceremonies and rituals, the use of herbs as medicaments was also widespread, and shamans in some cultures were essentially herbalists. There was perhaps a sizable number of herbs whose healing effects were due to actual physiological changes. Dr. Erwin H. Ackerknecht, a notable medical historian, estimated that as many as 25–50 percent of the herbs used were effective for organic, truly pharmacological reasons.* However, in spite of the actual medicinal value of some herbs, the rationale underlying their use was still superstitious. It was a common belief of the Indians that specific roots or plants were beneficial because they were distasteful and injurious to those spirits within the body causing the disease. Hence the use of foul-tasting medicines, such as emetics and purges, was extensive. The majority of herbs, though, were probably effective only insofar as they contributed to the shaman's repertoire.

Shamans relied heavily upon elaborate regalia, which in itself helped to create the ambience in which the shaman flourished. Andreas Lommel, an expert on shamanism, asserted that the shaman was basically an artistically creative man. Lommel also postulated that shamanism originated in early hunting cultures and that the paraphernalia of the shaman represented an animal disguise.

Dr. Michael Gelfand, who has lived and practiced medicine in South Africa for many years, described the *nganga* of the Shona people in Rhodesia, and of other African cultures as well. According to Gelfand, the *nganga* is the African embodiment of the shaman, herbalist, diviner or healer and has imprecisely been called a witch doctor. Gelfand referred to the *nganga* as the "artist *par excellence.* He uses every means—dress, amulets, beads, incantations and rituals—to impress his clients and win their confidence, and in

---

* Significant portions of the following discussion are derived from the work of Drs. Erwin H. Ackerknecht, Michael Gelfand, Kivuto Ndeti, Kamuti Kiteme and Jerome D. Frank.

this respect he is an unqualified success." Amulets, worn suspended from the neck or waist by a string, are frequently seen in African cultures. An amulet may simply consist of a small twig, a seed of a particular plant, or a piece of root, and it is believed to exert definite curative effects. Amulets are also worn for their preventive value, either to confer good fortune to the wearer or to prevent the entry of evil. There is a wide diversity of these objects, which are associated with healing effects. They are prescribed liberally by African doctors, in some cultures, for a multitude of personal and medical problems, including headaches, lovemaking, stomachaches, blindness and search for wealth.

Dr. Kamuti Kiteme of City College of the City University of New York discussed the efficacy of the entire procedure, which is dependent upon complex psychological processes. The doctor's "word" is far more potent than the "medicine" per se, and this enables the doctor to redefine the healing power of any given object, or amulet, in the therapy of entirely different diseases. Gelfand expressed a similar view in his description of the African medicine man's use of "suggestive therapy." While some herbs may have scientific validity, the majority of cures are effected through suggestion. The whole setting which is created by the African medicine man (the special attire, the incantations, his knowledge of herbs, and observance of certain taboos) makes an impact upon the patient. The rituals and regalia contribute to an aura of mystery and skill, conveying the impression of wisdom passed down through the generations. The medicine man who is imbued with all of these qualities holds the confidence of his patients, who are psychologically very susceptible to treatment.

Ultimately, the advantages of psychological therapy can be attributed to the doctor-patient relationship. The relationship between the *nganga* and the Shona people of Rhodesia, for example, is based upon esteem, affection and sympathy. There is a qualitative difference between this type of interaction and the style of the European or Western doctor, which is often less personal. The superiority in psychological understanding attained by the *nganga*, which is often discounted by the more scientifically oriented doctors, should instead be emulated.

Dr. Jerome D. Frank, Professor of Psychiatry at Johns Hopkins University, analyzed features of healing procedures in primitive societies. He concluded that the healing effects of these procedures derive from the patient's expectation of help. This expectation of help, which can operate as a powerful healing force, has also been referred to as "expectant trust." The patient's expectation of help results partially from the healer's personal attributes or magnetism. It is engendered primarily through the paraphernalia of the healer, which itself is effective insofar as its symbolic meaning has been culturally determined.

Frank briefly accounted for the recent substantial following of disreputable cults, noting that the success of such charlatans is also based upon the ability to evoke the patient's expectancy of help. The healer figure in these various cultic groups is comparable to the shaman in that he is perceived as the transmitter of awesome healing powers. Frank concluded that "the apparent success of healing methods based on all sorts of ideologies and methods compels the conclusion that the healing power of faith resides in the patient's state of mind, not in the validity of its object."

The fundamental dichotomy between the mind and the body, which modern Western civilization seems unable to reject, simply does not exist in primitive societies. Ackerknecht indicated that the strength of primitive medicine derives from the unity of life and thought and he referred to the "unitarian or total character of primitive medicine . . . Magic or religion seems to satisfy better than any other device a certain eternal psychic or 'metaphysical' need of mankind, sick and healthy, for integration and harmony." Frank stated that the duties of the shaman included "not only the administration of therapeutic agents but provision of means for confession, atonement, restoration into the good graces of family and tribe, and intercession with the spirit world. The shaman's role may thus involve aspects of the roles of physician, magician, priest, moral arbiter, representative of the group's world-view, and agent of social control." Perhaps the shaman's work represents a viable model for definition of the appropriate functions of a good modern doctor.

However, it appears that medicine in the Western world, which was once an integration of both science

65

and art, has shifted to an emphasis on science at the expense of art. Ackerknecht asserted that "it is safe to state as a further general characteristic of primitive medicine that it is primarily magico-religious, utilizing a few rational elements; while our medicine is predominantly rational and scientific, employing a few magic elements."

Modern medicine has abandoned many of the useless and sometimes dangerous superstitious practices. The current approach to medical therapies, however, with its emphasis on scientific quantification, has led to professional disdain for many of the beneficial, nonspecific elements of treatment. These nonspecific factors do play an important role in healing. The Rev. Dr. Randall C. Mason, Jr., of the Seabury-Western and Chicago Theological Seminaries, Dr. Graham Clark and the Rev. Robert B. Reeves, Jr., of Columbia University and the Rev. S. Bruce Wagner of the Nassau (N.Y.) Council of Churches investigated "the speed of healing" in forty-six patients who suffered from detachment of their retinas. All patients had their attitudes rated by a chaplain prior to corrective eye surgery. Preoperative ratings of each patient's attitude were obtained. The ratings included such factors as reaction to the illness; the patient's trust in the surgeon; optimism concerning outcome; reaction to a chaplain; confidence in ability to cope; ability to do things independently; and other similar factors. An "Acceptance Scale" was derived from these evaluations. After the surgery was performed, a surgeon rated the speed of healing. The surgeon and chaplain, performing their respective ratings, avoided conversations about the patients so that they would not influence each other's judgments. The results clearly demonstrated that the degree of "acceptance" was related to the speed of healing. The authors concluded that:

> ... high acceptance and rapid healing occur, despite the psychological make-up of the person or the intensity of the threat, when the patient has faith in the healer, his methods of healing, and feels that these methods are relevant to the cause of his illness. Low acceptance and poor healing occur when such beliefs are undermined. Furthermore ... the person seeking to help the slow healer should not be concerned with either the intrapsychic make-up of the patient (which may take years to change) or with environmental factors. Rather, he should focus primarily on what variables enhance or destroy the patient's attitude of expectant faith.

I am not in any sense advocating the use of superstition, rituals or exorcism. Although all these beliefs have affected spiritual aspects of human life and may certainly contain legitimate elements, they have represented an impediment to the advancement of scientific medicine in many areas of the world. For example, the African *nganga* can be credited with the discovery of various herbal remedies which are of substantial medicinal value. His expertise in treating simple psychological disturbances through suggestion should not be underestimated. Despite these contributions, his presence medically is seen as a handicap. Gelfand stated that the *nganga* today constitutes a great obstacle to scientific progress. His final assessment of the *nganga* is sobering: "The *nganga* is the hub round which the spiritual world revolves, and so long as he functions as a dispenser of antidotes to witchcraft, so long will the African's bondage to fear continue." Indeed, to adopt today the practices of native medicine would only serve to hinder medical progress. Rather, I feel that primitive medicine serves as a good model to understand better the significant nonspecific factors of medical treatment.

Perhaps the very different approaches which characterize modern medicine and primitive medicine are best used complementarily. Dr. Kivuto Ndeti of the University of Nairobi maintained:

> It would be a wise move for scientific medicine to meet tradition half-way . . . This also applies to the relation between the witch doctor and his modern counterpart . . . Therapies and treatments performed by witch doctors should be examined critically and the relevant elements should be adopted into modern education. They touch many vital areas which are beyond the imagination of the present medical education and they are wholesome in approach. This is a virtue which modern medical science cannot afford to condemn.

These relevant, nonspecific treatment factors of traditional medicine have been largely dismissed in modern medicine.

4

THE NONSPECIFIC TREATMENT aspects of traditional medicine have been termed *placebos* and *placebo effects*. The placebo effect must be differentiated from the placebo. A standard definition of placebo, as stated in *Dorland's Illustrated Medical Dictionary*, is:

> an inactive substance or preparation given to satisfy the patient's symbolic need for drug therapy and used in controlled studies to determine the efficacy of medicinal substances. Also, a procedure with no intrinsic therapeutic value, performed for such purposes.

However, the significance of the placebo has been minimized by such a narrow definition. Recognizing the potential benefits of nonspecific factors in any treatment procedure, Dr. Arthur K. Shapiro of the Payne-Whitney Psychiatric Clinic at New York Hospital has adopted a broader view of the placebo. He describes the placebo as any treatment (or any part of a treatment) which does not have a *specific* action on the patient's symptoms or disease but which nonetheless may have an effect upon the patient. Placebos may be given deliberately by the physician for such an effect. Various *nonspecific* elements of treatment, such as the therapeutic setting and the doctor's presence, may also be viewed as placebos. I prefer to adopt this latter, more general definition of placebo. The traditionally negative connotation of the word placebo must not prevent us from recognizing the potential benefits of the nonspecific factors associated with placebos.

The placebo effect, then, may be defined as the changes in the patient, symptom or disease produced by placebos. A placebo effect, as Shapiro points out, "may or may not occur or may be favorable or unfavorable." *I am not, in any sense, endorsing a physician's use of traditional placebos, such as injections of salt water and administration of sugar pills. I believe their use to be dishonest and unethical. They should have little place in the practice of medicine. The use of deception in both clinical and experimental medicine is, in my opinion, unacceptable. Rather, I refer to the nonspecific features of therapy and propose that their positive use might benefit the practice of modern medicine.*

The attitude of disdain for the placebo effect can be traced to the introduction of controlled pharmacological investigations of the 1950s. These controlled investigations were designed to test the efficacy of new drugs. For example, a new "active" drug, called Drug A, is thought to be effective in treating a medical problem, such as tension headaches. Theoretically, any new drug could alleviate tension headaches. However, improvement in the patient's headaches might be due to the nonspecific factor of increased medical attention necessitated by the testing procedures, and not due to a specific action of the new drug, Drug A.

To ascertain whether Drug A is indeed effective, a control group is necessary. The control group should be given another agent, let us say Drug B, which is known to be ineffective for tension headaches. A sugar pill is such an example and has been called a placebo. If the experiment is properly conducted, patients will be divided into two groups which are similar with respect to frequency and severity of tension headaches, age, sex and as many other personal characteristics as possible. One of the groups should be given "active" Drug A; the other group should receive the placebo, Drug B. Both groups should receive the same number of pills per day, and both Drug A and Drug B should look exactly alike. Both groups of patients should also be asked the same questions and should be given an equal amount of attention. Thus, the patient does not know whether he or she has received the allegedly active Drug A or the placebo, Drug B. The patient is "blind" to the possible chemical action of either drug. Since the expectancy of the investigator may also play a role in the results, the investigator should not know which patient is receiving which drug. Both Drug A and Drug B should be packaged before the investigation; one set should be allotted to one group and the other, seemingly identical, set to the second group. The actual identity of Drugs A and B would only be known by an individual not involved in the administration of the drugs or in the assessment of their effects. The investigator would therefore also be "blind"; he or she would not know which drug was issued to which group.

This type of experiment is an example of a "double-blind-controlled" investigation. It is double-blind since both the investigator and the patient do not know which is the active agent; it is controlled since the experimental design includes a control group. At the end of the investigation, both Drug A and Drug B are found to be effective in 50–60 percent of the patients suffering from tension headaches. Since there is no significant difference between Drug A and Drug B in the relief of tension headaches, Drug A is usually not considered to be a useful agent because it was no more effective than the placebo, Drug B. This method of searching for effective drugs has been very successful in the introduction of new, active medications. Controlled investigations attempt to evaluate unwarranted, often fraudulent, claims of success. Most of the drugs prescribed by physicians have been subjected to such testing, and present medical practice relies heavily upon the use of active drugs.

We noted that Drug A and Drug B were equally efficacious and concluded that Drug A was no more useful than a placebo. To find relief for tension headaches, the standard procedure in the testing of new drugs has been to start over with a different drug, Drug C, and so on, until a drug more effective than the placebo is found. However, if a drug that is "inactive" (such as both Drugs A and B in our example) alleviates the pain of tension headaches, should we not pay more attention to the factors which have contributed to this relief? Should we ignore the fact that Drug A is 50–60 percent successful in reducing tension headaches? After all, we have attained the desired result, the relief of pain. Why should we search for another drug, if the placebo effect has produced a valuable result in a sizable percentage of patients? We should further investigate the components of the placebo effect so that its use can lead to better health.

The placebo effect appears to result from a combination of factors involving the patient, the physician and the relationship between the two.* Of utmost importance is a meaningful doctor-patient interaction, which enables the transfer of the patient's concerns to an acknowledged scientist and healer, the physician. For example, a favorable placebo effect may commence before the actual administra-

---

* Significant portions of the discussion of the placebo effect are from collaborative work with Mark D. Epstein, currently a student at Harvard Medical School.

tion of a pill. If the patient reacts adversely to a therapeutic encounter, symptoms can be made worse and the patient may develop anxiety.

The effectiveness of both active and inactive drugs can be influenced by the psychological state of the patient. Patients who are anxious about their illness and endure much discomfort experience more relief from an inactive, or inert, pill than do nonanxious patients. Also, a patient who believes that the treatment will be effective is much more likely to benefit from it.

Dr. Stewart Wolf, in 1950, while at New York Hospital, clearly demonstrated the potency of patient expectation in experiments employing ipecac. Ipecac causes nausea and vomiting by acting upon specific areas of the brain, and also by directly irritating the stomach. It is frequently used to induce vomiting in cases of drug overdoses. Wolf measured stomach contractions through use of a small balloon, swallowed by the patient, which was attached to recording devices. When the stomach contracted it would squeeze the balloon and the pressure changes in the balloon were then recorded. Normally, the stomach has periodic contractions; decreased stomach contractions are associated with nausea and vomiting. The ingestion of ipecac leads to decreased contractions. One of Wolf's patients was suffering from the nausea and vomiting often experienced during pregnancy. He had her swallow such a balloon. Decreased stomach contractions were recorded as was anticipated. The subject was then told she would receive a medication which would abolish her nausea when, in fact, she was given the drug ipecac. The subject's normal stomach contractions returned following the ingestion of ipecac. She did not experience nausea again until the next morning. The patient's expectation of a specific drug action led to the reversal of its "true" pharmacological action.

Not only are the patient's attitude, anxieties or expectations influential in affecting treatment outcome; the thoughts and behavior of the physician have a profound effect. Physicians who are self-confident, are attentive to the needs of the patient and have faith in the effectiveness of the treatments they are offering are more likely to induce positive health changes through the placebo effect. Understanding and acceptance by the physician, as well as frequently scheduled visits, are also important for the improvement of the patient. Physicians who interact with their patients in a warm and friendly manner will contribute to a positive placebo effect. Hippocrates, the fifth/fourth-century B.C. Greek physician who has been called the Father of Modern Medicine, clearly understood the significance of this phenomenon. He said: "For some patients, though conscious that their condition is perilous, recover their health simply through their contentment with the goodness of the physician."

The attitudes of both the physician and the patient are important factors contributing to the placebo effect. However, the *interaction between the physician and the patient* is probably the most important factor. The placebo effect probably derives most of its power from the great potential of the emotional relationship between the physician and the patient. If there is a good doctor-patient relationship, and if there is consistency between the patient's and physician's expectations concerning the treatment, the chances are maximized for improvement in the patient's health due to nonspecific treatment elements. When the physician's approach is not in accordance with the patient's expectations of treatment and the patient's attitude toward his or her illness, as when the patient denies illness, a positive placebo effect is not likely to occur. When, however, the patient feels comfortable revealing himself or herself to the physician, especially during the medical history-taking, the doctor can more clearly understand the important developmental and situational aspects of the patient's life. In this way, a satisfying and helpful doctor-patient relationship can be formed and will aid the total treatment process. Indeed, one of the essential aspects of the "art of medicine" is a good doctor-patient relationship.

The environment in which the patient receives his therapy can also affect the outcome of that therapy. A trip to the doctor's office with the intention of being provided treatment can improve health, as can transferring a person from the setting in which he has incurred, or suffered a major part of, his illness. Moreover, the type of therapeutic situation influences receptivity to treatment. An investigative setting may have beneficial effects on the health of a patient. In one medical study it was found that the increased attention given to schizophrenic patients by a special research unit resulted in the improvement of approximately 80 percent of these patients. This finding is comparable to the "Hawthorne effect," whereby the additional attention given to factory workers during an investigation improved the efficiency of the workers.

On the other hand, drugs administered in surroundings which upset or confuse the patient may result in these drugs having a paradoxical effect, or an effect contrary to that expected. In one study, normal subjects were given either a tranquilizing drug or a placebo, preceding a stressful psychiatric interview. The subjects did not know what they were receiving. The physiological sensations induced by the tranquilizing drugs, particularly morphine and chlorpromazine, were interpreted as threatening by the subjects. Hence, in the stressful experimental setting, the drugs exerted an anxiety-provoking effect, instead of their supposed tranquilizing effect, on the central nervous system. The physiological changes which are generally associated with decreased anxiety were in fact accompanied by a subjective report of increased anxiety. The environmental setting in which a drug is taken is extremely important, as it may intensify, decrease or even reverse the expected drug action. This phenomenon helps to explain why alcohol taken in solitude may be a depressant, whereas alcohol taken in a social context may act as a stimulant.

We have seen that inert pills, saline injections and a whole host of nonspecific treatment elements may exert a powerful therapeutic influence. However, in discussing the role of the placebo and the placebo effect in medicine, we must not fail to weigh their benefits against their negative aspects. Like all potent tools in medical practice, both the specific placebo regimens and the nonspecific elements of treatment have the potential to harm. An exceptional physician and researcher, the late Dr. Henry K. Beecher of Harvard Medical School, discussed the toxicity of supposedly innocuous placebo injections and tablets. He described a number of symptoms reported by patients who had taken placebo tablets. Among these symptoms were drowsiness, headaches, difficulty in concentrating, nausea, dryness of the mouth, a sensation of heaviness, relaxation and fatigue. Others have noted rashes, itching, swelling of the lips, palpitations, abdominal cramps, constipation and diarrhea after placebo administration.

Several other investigators have shown that the nonspecific elements of treatment such as the therapeutic setting and the doctor-patient interaction can also have negative effects. An unfriendly relationship between doctor and patient may be injurious to both parties. A patient who distrusts his physician may not be truthful about his medical history, or the patient may fail to follow the doctor's medical advice. Doctors must be attuned to their patients' psychological and sociological needs and understand the context in which their patients live and work. Also, a physician who feels hostile or resentful toward a patient may find his professional skill and judgment impaired.

A lack of communication between the doctor and patient is also potentially harmful. A physician who does not offer a patient an adequate explanation of his illness invites misinterpretation and misunderstanding. A patient may think that the doctor, by omitting details of his condition, is concealing a horrible truth from him, possibly to spare anguish. Another type of miscommunication involves the patient's responses to conversations accidentally overheard. Dr. Robert T. Corney, a psychiatrist at the University of Virginia School of Medicine, cites two cases in which patients, before losing total consciousness during anesthesia, heard negative remarks by their physicians. The inadvertent remarks caused these individuals great psychological distress.

These examples indeed demonstrate that any negative aspects of therapy, whether they are specific interventions or the nonspecific elements, may jeopardize the health of a patient. Dr. J. N. G. Davidson, a physician from New Zealand, once stated: "Let us remember then, the power for good, or for harm, not only of the drugs we put in our patients' bodies; but also—and of far greater importance—of the power for good, or harm, of the ideas and emotions we induce, wittingly or unwittingly, in our patients' minds."

In its present disregard for the *positive* placebo

effect, medicine has lost a valuable asset, an asset which sustained it for centuries. Such a beneficial element should be reincorporated into medicine. The potential value of nonspecific factors should not be underestimated but must be recognized as a potent and versatile tool. Indeed, neglecting to use the positive placebo effect to its fullest advantage is the poor practice of medicine. The following chapters will demonstrate specifically how modern medicine, through disregard of the basic elements which constitute the placebo effect, is sacrificing an important asset in the treatment of patients and is leading to excessive costs and even to ill health.

MEDICINE HAS MADE truly wondrous progress in recent decades. Modern medicine has effectively eliminated many of the scourges which have afflicted mankind throughout history. In the Western world today, the diseases of plague, cholera, smallpox and polio are essentially nonexistent. Children can be expected to live to adulthood; it is rare to lose a child to disease. Appendicitis is no longer life threatening. Pneumonia, once a dire disease, is now curable. Syphilis, which has killed and maimed millions in the past, is also curable. Diabetes can be controlled with insulin. Pernicious anemia, a fatal disease which mimics a cancer of the blood, can be alleviated by administration of vitamin B_{12}. Pellagra, a very serious disease primarily affecting the skin, the digestive organs and the nervous system, has been recognized as a nutritional deficiency. It can be cured by increasing the intake of specific vitamins. Surgery can now be performed with reasonable safety and effectiveness on any organ of the body, although as recently as World War II the heart, for example, was considered to be an inoperable organ. Sophisticated surgical and medical technologies enable the repair of extensive injuries which, unattended, would be fatal. Sight and hearing can be restored to some of those who would have been permanently blind and deaf.

These advances in medical science are reflected in health statistics. A person born in the United States in 1900 could expect to live an average of 49.2 years, whereas in 1975 the average life expectancy at birth had risen to 72.5 years. This increase in life expectancy is due mainly to the reduction in infant and child mortality. As reported by the U.S. Bureau of the Census, 61.9 out of every 1000 male infants born alive in 1940 died before they reached 1 year of age. In 1975 this number decreased to 18.3 out of every 1000 male infants. Moreover, there has been a major decline in the death rate for male children between 1 and 5 years: 0.31 percent died in 1940 whereas 0.07 percent died in 1974. Corresponding decreases in mortality have occurred in female infants and children.

Despite the progress medicine has made, many people are dissatisfied with present health care. They feel that medicine is not meeting their needs and that it is exorbitantly expensive. Although the reasons for this dissatisfaction are multifaceted, the dissatisfaction may be analyzed and explained within the framework of the placebo effect. The placebo effect, as noted previously, is dependent upon a combination of factors involving the patient, the physician and the relationship between the two. What a patient expects from health care determines to a great extent his or her subsequent reaction to a medical encounter. Realistic expectations are conducive to a positive placebo effect. However, the phenomenal medical advances, achieved through the application of scientific methods, are partially responsible for making people expect too much. These medical advances have accelerated in the last thirty years starting with the introduction of the antibiotic agents such as penicillin. However, modern medicine has not been able to eliminate aging, disease and death. People tend to believe that all illness may be prevented and cured. This is not a realistic expectation. We cannot stay young or feel young indefinitely; we all must die. We become afflicted with illnesses that may not have been prevented and for which there may be no cure. They must be accepted as part of our lives. Since people are no longer forced to deal with the dread diseases of polio, smallpox, typhus and diphtheria, they feel that they should not have to cope with pains or signs of aging. People believe that it is only a matter of time before all forms of cancer, heart and lung disease and, by implication, death itself are eradicated. This is an extraordinarily foolish expectation! As Peter Mere Latham, the nineteenth-century English physician, said: "Physicians, who have worthily achieved great reputation, become the refuge of the hopeless, and earn for themselves the misfortune of being expected to cure incurable diseases." If we were not susceptible to disease and death, we would not be human. One can reasonably expect, however, that medicine should keep people as healthy as possible for as long as possible.

Modern medicine, perhaps due to its own scientific progress, is disregarding one of its most essential elements, the placebo effect. As has been previously discussed, modern medicine has come to scorn the placebo effect with the acceptance of experimental designs such as those employed in testing the efficacy of new drugs. In its justifiable adherence to scientific method, medicine has overlooked traditional, nonspecific healing practices. It is difficult to establish the worth of these nonspecific practices by using currently accepted scientific methodology. However, it is unwise to disregard these worthwhile treatment elements simply because they are not easily investigated.

MEDICAL TRAINING

Medical schools are required to teach the vast body of knowledge based upon scientific approaches, even though much of this knowledge is in a rather incomplete state. The new scientific "facts" proliferate at an ever increasing pace. In order to keep abreast of these scientific advances, medical students and physicians require so much training that the beneficial factors inherent in the doctor-patient relationship are given only token attention. Dr. William J. Mayo, one of the founders of Minnesota's Mayo Clinic, remarked: "One meets with many men who have been fine students, and have stood high in their classes, who have great knowledge of medicine but very little wisdom in application. They have mastered the science, and have failed in the understanding of the human being."

People starting their careers in medicine are often motivated by humanitarian reasons. They wish to help people and to gain the attendant personal satisfactions. Early in their training, these concerns for the patient remain quite active. The unquestionable importance of acquiring medical expertise, however, necessitates concentration upon the technology of medicine at the expense of learning how to relate to patients.

Although the significance of the doctor-patient relationship has been emphasized by some physicians, little has been done to restructure medical education accordingly. A few programs, courses and seminars have been introduced to improve medical students' understanding of their own and of their patients' feelings, or to improve communication between doctor and patient. The attempts to encourage medical students to spend more time on courses emphasizing the "whole" patient have not been successful because, as Dr. Bernard Barber of Columbia University suggests, these courses are not taken seriously by many faculty members whose orientation is that of traditional science.

Moreover, although a basic knowledge of general medicine is acquired in medical school, the diagnosis, discussion and treatment of esoteric, rare diseases are considered more exciting than the diagnosis and management of the common ailments. More recognition is given to students for the diagnosis and subsequent management of a rare disease than for that of a more prevalent illness. Dr. Leon Eisenberg, Professor of Psychiatry at Harvard Medical School, believes that although most patients seen by a physician suffer from relatively minor illnesses, the training of these physicians was conducted "in a university hospital and its clinics, where the proportions of minor and serious illness are reversed."*

This observation is supported by the Cleveland Family Study, in which Dr. John H. Dingle of the Western Reserve University School of Medicine studied a highly selected population of families for a ten-year period, with respect to the occurrence of illness. From January 1948 to May 1957, the incidence of illness in eighty-six families, which consisted of 443 individuals, was recorded. The families were of middle or upper socioeconomic status. At the time of admission to the investigation, the median age of the mothers was 30, and that of the fathers, 33. The health status of each family member was

---

* Significant portions of the following discussion are derived from a compilation of articles edited by Dr. John H. Knowles, President of the Rockefeller Foundation.

determined by a medical interview (a history), physical examination, chest x-ray and blood and urine tests. The overall health of the population was regarded as excellent at the beginning of the study; no one was suffering from an incapacitating chronic disorder. Subsequent examinations were made at six-month intervals for the children and at one-year intervals for the adults. The mother in each family recorded the symptoms of any illness for the family members. Fieldworkers visited the homes weekly to discuss these records. When an ailment was considered not to be trivial, a staff physician made a visit to the home and treated the ill member of the family. The physicians and fieldworkers diagnosed every illness which had been recorded by the mothers. At the end of the ten years, a total of 25,155 illnesses was diagnosed, that is, an average of 9.4 illnesses per person per year. This number was heavily influenced by the high illness rate of young children. "Common respiratory diseases," consisting chiefly of common colds, but also including rhinitis (inflammation of the mucous membranes of the nose), laryngitis and bronchitis, comprised 60 percent of all illnesses diagnosed. "Specific respiratory illnesses," such as streptococcal infections, pneumonia and influenza, accounted for only 3 percent of all illnesses. These percentages are important because most of the common respiratory illnesses should be treated with the supportive measures of rest, increased fluids and aspirin. In contrast, the less frequently occurring specific respiratory illnesses require the administration of special drugs, such as the antibiotics.

Similar findings were reported by physicians in England. Dr. Keith Hodgkin, a general practitioner in Yorkshire, noted that the majority of patients he encountered suffered from respiratory and mental diseases, problems rarely encountered in his hospital training. As a medical student and intern most of the patients he saw suffered from malignant, gastrointestinal and cardiovascular diseases, problems not often seen later in his clinical practice. Over a period of fifteen years, Dr. John Fry, a general practitioner in London, observed that 68 percent of the patients he saw suffered from common diseases. He defined these as minor, self-limiting conditions, usually lasting less than three months, and unlikely to cause any permanent aftereffects. Diseases which lasted more than three years and left permanent disabilities comprised 27 percent of his patient population. Major diseases, "potential killers," constituted the remaining 5 percent of cases.

During the formative training years of a physician, the internship and residency, most exposure to patients occurs within a hospital setting. The patients seen are often quite ill and very dependent upon the expertise of the physician. The patient is frequently too ill to be made a responsive and responsible partner in the healing process. A physician therefore does not learn to make use of a positive placebo effect based upon a meaningful interaction between the physician and the patient.

Medical training emphasizes the knowledge of the latest material published in the medical journals. These articles generally describe small modifications in the diagnosis and management of various medical problems. "Missing" a rare diagnosis or being unaware of the most recently described procedures is often viewed as a sign of inadequate knowledge. Extensive diagnostic procedures and laboratory tests are then performed indiscriminately so that possible, although highly improbable, diseases are not overlooked. Too little time is spent training physicians to learn the basic components of management of a sick patient. Many of these components are the nonspecific treatment factors which are associated with a positive placebo effect.

Advances in medicine usually occur slowly. A seeming improvement or advancement is criticized and modified. It is therefore unwarranted to assume that the most recent publication contains the most valid, applicable information. Too often, the emphasis is placed upon the latest variation in the management of a disease even though it has not yet been fully verified. The belief in the superiority of novelty is partially enhanced by the inadequacy of current approaches to many medical problems. The inadequacy of management, in this sense, demands that a new approach be tried.

However, few analyses have been done to ascertain the relative values of both established and new procedures. Moreover, many of the new procedures have not been completely validated. Unvalidated procedures contribute to a waste of money and skilled services and their use can lead to serious diagnostic error. For example, the Wassermann diagnostic blood test for syphilis was widely used for forty years. Only recently was the test recognized to be overly sensitive. The test yielded false positive results. About one-half of the individuals who were told that they suffered from syphilis did not have this disease. These individuals needlessly underwent therapy which entailed considerable risk, including the possibility of being given hepatitis. They also unjustly suffered from the social stigma which is associated with venereal disease.

NEW TECHNOLOGIES

The concept of "definitive" and "half-way" technologies has recently been discussed. Definitive technologies, such as immunization, use of antibiotics and many forms of corrective surgery, are based upon extensive scientific research concerning disease processes and deal with the prevention, cure and control of disease. On the other hand, half-way technologies (surgery to relieve the blocked or partially blocked arteries that supply the heart muscle, the coronary arteries; renal dialysis; corrective orthopedic devices) can offer relief or partial correction, but not cure. Dr. Lewis Thomas, President of the Memorial Sloan-Kettering Cancer Center in New York City, emphasizes the need for definitive technologies in medicine, the safety and effectiveness of which have been determined before they are put into practice. Efforts should be directed toward research which would yield additional definitive technologies.

If there are no definitive technologies for the prevention or cure of a disease, it is unwarranted to expect the half-way technologies to be completely effective. Frequently, a search begins for newer and allegedly better techniques that may offer no additional advantages and are simply other half-way technologies. Disappointment is inevitable. Rather than beginning such a quest, which may worsen existing disease or create yet another ailment, the doctor and patient together should weigh the anticipated risks and benefits of each therapeutic step. A mutual decision should be made regarding an optimal course which takes into account the probable impact of the therapy on the total life of the patient.

The inclination to try the newest techniques has been capitalized upon by business interests. As stated by Dr. A. Paton, in a review of Ivan Illich's *Medical Nemesis:* "In an industrial society devoted to progress with a capital 'P,' there is no shortage of propagandists, both inside and outside the medical profession, who shout from rooftops, appropriately festooned with television aerials, the benefits and breakthroughs of modern technology."

Health-care expenditures in the United States have markedly increased. In 1929 approximately $3.5 billion, representing 3.6 percent of the Gross National Product, were spent in the United States for health care. In 1940 over $12 billion, or 4.5 percent of the Gross National Product were spent and in 1975 these expenditures rose to approximately $118.5 billion, or 8.2 percent of the Gross National Product. In 1929 each American spent an average of $29.16 for health services and supplies, including drugs, hospital fees and physician's services. In 1950 this amount increased to $78.35, whereas in 1975 it rose to $547.03. Although there is no single reason for this increase, the modifications in medical technology constitute one major factor. Dr. Ivan L. Bennett, Jr., Dean of the School of Medicine at New York University, maintains that the high cost of medical care is due to the use of half-way technologies. Definitive technologies, in contrast, are relatively less complex and less expensive.

New diagnostic instruments are often bought because they can perform more measurements more quickly. The efficiency of these modern machines is often predicated upon the fact that many different tests can be performed at the same time. The fallacy in this reasoning is that many of the tests done simultaneously are not needed for a given case. For example, although a physician may require only a specific measurement of one of the components of the blood's chemistry, it has become more expensive to obtain this one measurement than to obtain an entire battery of measurements. The argument is made that all the information gained is medically useful. However, this additional information leads to further tests since seeming abnormalities are frequently pursued. Thus these tests generate other tests. This is a highly profitable set of circumstances not only for the medical instrumentation industry but also for the medical profession.

The most insidious feature of this spiraling process is that a patient's individual identity assumes a lower priority. More attention is focused upon the technical laboratory findings than upon the patient. As Dr. William J. Mayo aptly stated in the early half of the twentieth century, "the highly scientific development of this mechanistic age has led perhaps to some loss in appreciation of the individuality of the patient and to trusting largely to the laboratories and outside agencies which tended to make the patient not the hub of the wheel, but a spoke." In recent years this tendency has become much more prevalent. The person becomes identified as his or her disease. "The myocardial infarction in room 121 is still complaining of chest pain." Thus the doctor-patient relationship is sharply fragmented. As Dr. Alex M. Burgess and his son, Dr. Alex M. Burgess, Jr., of Providence, Rhode Island, wrote in 1966: "Many of the old virtues seem to be neglected or lost. As a result of the mass of technical information that students and house officers are supposed to absorb, a breed of physicians who are capable medical scientists but poor doctors is coming into existence."

Medical students and physicians, however, cannot be held solely responsible for this unfortunate course of events. The acquisition of technical knowledge consumes a large amount of a student's and physician's time. New technical developments must be integrated with already existing practices. The result is less time readily available for direct communication with the patient or with the patient's family.

SPECIALIZATION

Another result of the ever increasing knowledge which physicians are required to attain has been the trend toward specialization. Since no one individual can be an expert in all fields, specialists have become common. In 1966 Dr. K. L. White of Johns Hopkins University estimated that there were fifty-four separate medical specialties and subspecialties, and the number has probably increased since that time. In 1973 over 76 percent of the physicians in the United States were specialists. Whereas there was one doctor for approximately every 700 people, there was only one "primary-care physician" for approximately every 4000 people. Dr. Henry Wechsler of Boston's Medical Foundation, Inc., has defined a primary-care physician as one involved in general practice, pediatrics, family practice or internal medicine. He has noted that the actual number of primary-care physicians has decreased even though the number of doctors has increased. In 1974 there were 859 fewer primary-care physicians than in 1964, a decrease of 1 percent. In the same decade the number of specialists had increased by 45,604, a change of 37 percent.

Unfortunately, the trend toward specialization tends to remove the patient from a meaningful doctor-patient relationship, since many physicians often take care of one individual. As Dr. R. B. Greenblatt of the Medical College of Georgia stated: "The emotional disenchantment between patient and physician started with the vanishing family doctor and the emergence of the specialist. Depth of personal understanding has yielded to breadth of medical knowledge."

In tracing the history of medical specialization, Dr. Robert H. Ebert, former Dean of Harvard Medical School, states that the benefits received by specialists practicing within the armed forces during World War II made the decline of the general practitioner inevitable. At this time specialists were given increased pay and better assignments, as well as higher rank. Moreover, as specialization became more lucrative, the pattern of medical education changed. Whereas previously, upon graduation, physicians entered general practice for several years before proceeding to a specialty field, this customary waiting period was eliminated. Instead, medical school graduates immediately entered specialty training. Presently, due to medical developments, social factors and government-sponsored training programs, the trend is toward "subspecialization"—neuro-surgery instead of general surgery and cardiology instead of internal medicine.

This specialization reinforces the concept of the mind-body dichotomy since it divides the body into organ systems. As has been previously noted, you cannot be compartmentalized into these arbitrary divisions. Medical specialization employing the newest technology indeed presents a lamentable situation for the patient, who needs to be treated as a whole person. As this trend toward specialization continues, we are rapidly losing the doctor-patient relationship and thus the potential for a positive placebo effect. Medical histories are being taken by computer and the physician is becoming less involved in the physical examination. In so fragmenting the doctor-patient relationship we have created a void in medical care. Have we not lost more than we have gained? We should not be surprised to find that modern medicine, with its potent interventions, has even contributed to ill health.

6

THE ANCIENT DICTUM, *primum non nocere* ("first of all do not harm"), generally attributed to Hippocrates, is the cornerstone of medicine. After all, what is more unacceptable of a physician than to make a patient more ill? As previously discussed, the physician had little to offer a patient, prior to the last century, other than the benefits of the placebo effect. For the patient who was not very ill, this would often suffice. Although the physician could confer the benefits of a positive placebo effect upon the more seriously ill patient, it was not sufficient to significantly alter the course of the disease. Specific treatment made little difference except to make the patient's illness worse or to cause another illness. In the twentieth century the very ill patient has, for the first time, a better than even chance of benefiting from an encounter with a physician. However, does our modern medical system help the person who is not seriously ill but who suffers from a rather poorly defined sickness? How well does our current medical approach succeed in the prevention of disease, or in the cure of definable illnesses? Can our success rate be improved and the potential for creating more illness lessened?

RISK VERSUS BENEFIT

The underlying principle that should be applied is that of the risk versus benefit ratio. The risks of the diagnosis and treatment of a disease should be weighed against the benefits to be expected from these procedures. If a disease is not suspected or is minor and poses little discomfort, it would be foolhardy to expose a patient to medical procedures which pose risks. The risk of the therapy then exceeds the benefits to be expected. Under such a circumstance, why should one be exposed to these risks? Dr. Louis Lasagna of Johns Hopkins University believes that "Given a choice between no treatment and effective treatment with a risk of toxicity, the modern physician must usually pick the latter. To paraphrase Emerson, it is the fertile soil, not the barren, which breeds fevers, crocodiles, tigers, and scorpions."

Further, patients are guilty of exposing themselves to excessive risks. An example of such a case is that of a 35-year-old business executive who, experiencing no medical symptoms, was referred to a prominent hospital for coronary arteriography to supplement his annual "executive check-up." Coronary arteriography is an x-ray procedure used to assess whether the arteries, or blood vessels, carrying blood to the heart muscle are obstructed. Special dye is injected into these coronary arteries to make them visible on x-ray. In the diagnosis of patients who suffer from heart disease or whose symptoms strongly suggest the presence of clogged arteries, this procedure is often necessary to better understand and treat the condition. However, the arteriography procedure may produce various complications such as heart attacks, markedly irregular heartbeating, blood clots requiring surgical removal and bleeding, in approximately 4 percent of cases. It is associated with death in about 0.5 percent (one-half of 1 percent) of patients undergoing this procedure.

Coronary arteriography was requested so that the executive be given the "latest and best" that medical science had to offer, despite the fact that he had no symptoms. He had already undergone his annual examination, which included a medical history, physical examination, blood and urine tests, an electrocardiogram and x-rays of the chest and bowel. The executive reasoned that he was "entitled" to know about the condition of his coronary arteries. Most American males have some blockage of their heart vessels in middle age. However, the surgical treatment available is unthinkable in the absence of symptoms. There was little benefit to be gained from undergoing this purely diagnostic procedure, which carries a small but recognized risk of death or serious complications. The initial hospital refused to do this procedure. The executive was not satisfied and went to several other hospitals until arteriography was finally performed; he was told that he had no significant obstruction. The executive fortunately escaped any damage from the procedure. Today, several years later, and still without symptoms, he is demanding to have coronary arteriography repeated for his own reassurance. He will again find someone to perform the procedure and will further increase his chances of developing medical complications.

On the other hand, if a person has signs and symptoms indicative of a serious disease that can be treated, procedures that carry substantial risks are warranted. A 45-year-old man was in excellent health until he injured his leg in a fall while jogging. His leg subsequently became painful, red and swollen. The diagnosis of thrombophlebitis was made. Thrombophlebitis, or inflammation of veins, is a serious disorder since the inflammation can lead to blood clots. The blood clots may break loose from the inflamed veins. Blood clots which are carried in the blood stream are called emboli. The clots may travel to the heart and then to the lungs. These clots, or pulmonary emboli, if very large, may block the arteries of the lung. Rapid death usually occurs, because blood can no longer pass through the lungs and obtain oxygen. While in the hospital, this patient suddenly developed chest pain and shortness of breath. Soon after, he lost consciousness. After other possible causes of these symptoms were ruled out, the diagnosis of a large pulmonary embolus was made. Under these emergency circumstances, immediate surgery was warranted. The surgery, although extremely risky, had the potential of saving the patient's life. The operation was successful and the patient subsequently recovered. If the surgery had contributed to the demise of the patient, it would still have been worth the risk, for the patient would certainly have died without it. In this case, the possible benefits outweighed the great risks.

Between these rather extreme examples in which the risk versus benefit ratio could be easily determined, there is a myriad of situations which require wise judgmental decisions. The ability to make sound decisions constitutes one aspect of the "art of medicine." Physicians must constantly weigh the risks of their actions against the potential benefits.

Both patients and physicians carry their expectations and beliefs into their interaction. Patients hope to have their complaints attended to and their discomforts and diseases alleviated. What a doctor is able to do, however, is often limited. In attempting to fulfil a patient's unrealistic expectations, a physician may perform tests and procedures and prescribe medicines which are superfluous. A physician who does not write a prescription for a patient suffering from an ailment and who does not order tests is frequently considered to be inadequate by the patient. Further, it may be anxiety-producing for the physician himself to do nothing. To "do something" is what is most often taught in medical school. To watch and wait in cases which do not require immediate action is rarely taught and is often considered to represent a lack of knowledge. Dr. Lasagna has noted that "there is unfortunately a 'furor therapeuticus' in many physicians which demands that every symptom be treated (almost at the spinal reflex level) by administration of a drug." The needless prescriptions and tests have often replaced the worthwhile aspects of the doctor-patient relationship. The interaction between a doctor and patient should enable the patient to express anxieties and fears as well as to raise questions about his or her state of health. This interaction has largely been replaced by tests and procedures. A multitude of tests are performed by specialized technicians, who, although competent, may take a less personal interest in the patient than does the patient's own physician. This is not progress, but rather an over-emphasis upon modern technology at the expense of time-proven approaches. Not only is this shift of emphasis needless, but it may also *cause* disease, which has been termed "iatrogenic" disease.

IATROGENESIS

Iatrogenic, from the Greek words *iatros* (physician) and *gennan* (to produce), may be defined as resulting from the actions of physicians. Originally the term referred to disorders induced in the patient as a result of the physician's examination, manner or discussion. That is, iatrogenic ailments were those precipitated by a physician who was not sufficiently aware of his patient's anxiety or of the effects of his words and actions upon the patient. The word iatrogenic is now applied to *any* adverse condition or illness which is engendered by the physician. Indeed, for centuries the physician's power to harm has been recognized. Latham was aware of this potential when he said: "Among the perils of disease we must not refuse to reckon the errors of physicians."

The frequency of iatrogenic disease in modern medicine is substantially increasing. The number of drugs and procedures, both diagnostic and therapeutic, utilized by the medical profession has increased substantially. As has been discussed, this proliferation has had many magnificent consequences. Millions of lives have been saved or prolonged, and those with incurable diseases have been made much more comfortable. We can no longer state, as did Dr. Oliver Wendell Holmes, the physician and man of letters, in 1860: "Throw out opium ... throw out a few specifics which our art did not discover ... throw out wine ... I firmly believe that if the whole materia medica, *as now used,* could be sunk to the bottom of the sea it would be all the better for mankind,—and all the worse for the fishes." Unfortunately, the recent contributions of medicine have been coupled with great increases in the number of adverse complications directly attributable to drugs and diagnostic and therapeutic procedures. The potent drugs and effective equipment used today possess a far greater potentiality to harm. The iatrogenic reactions, as noted by Dr. J. F. Gwynne of the University of Otago in New Zealand, "[vary] in severity from the trivial and transient to the irreversible and fatal." Discretion must be exercised in drug usage to avoid possible dangers.

Whereas historically the surgeon was largely responsible for the majority of the iatrogenic complications, the medical doctor prescribing drugs has recently become the main perpetrator of iatrogenic death and disease. Today the most common iatrogenic occurrences are those resulting from the use of drugs. We are in the midst of a "pharmacologic revolution," a "chemical age," or a state of affairs called "polypharmacy." In the 1978 *Physicians' Desk Reference* (*PDR*), the most commonly used source of drug information, there are over 1200 different generic drugs listed. There are over 5000 brand names by which these generic drugs are marketed.

Iatrogenic reactions leading to death, especially those related to drugs, have reached alarming proportions. In a report published in 1975, Dr. Nelson S. Irey of the Armed Forces Institute of Pathology estimated that between 6000 and 12,000 deaths occur annually in the United States from adverse drug reactions. The tragedy of this situation is that many of these deaths are unnecessary, since we are overusing drugs. If the risk versus benefit principle were appropriately applied, drug usage would be decreased.

We are not only inflicting injury upon ourselves, but also upon our offspring. The human fetus is particularly susceptible to drugs. The iatrogenic effects upon the developing fetus render a number of drugs unsafe during pregnancy. Since pregnancy in its early stages may not be recognized, a physician may prescribe harmful drugs to a pregnant woman. The probability of such an occurrence is increased because these agents are so commonly used.

Between 3 and 5 percent of a general practitioner's patients consult him because of iatrogenic drug complications which ultimately require admission to a hospital. Most of the adverse side effects occur within the gastrointestinal tract, although virtually any part of the body may be affected. The most typical symptoms and signs are nausea, vomiting, diarrhea, constipation, pain, jaundice and bleeding. The nature of these adverse reactions is of course determined by the type of drug used and its action.

Most investigations of the iatrogenic drug problem report that between 10 and 30 percent of patients already in a hospital develop an adverse drug reaction. In one study, Dr. Leighton E. Cluff, Dr. George F. Thornton and Dr. Larry G. Seidl of Johns Hopkins University found that 15 percent of the patients at that major medical center experienced iatrogenic effects from drugs. These doctors defined an adverse drug reaction as "any adverse response to medication undesired or unintended by the physician." In another study, Dr. Elihu M. Schimmel of Yale University reported that over 10 percent of patients hospitalized experienced deleterious complications associated with the administration of drugs.

Since hospitalization usually involves not only more drug usage but also more diagnostic tests and procedures, iatrogenic reactions are more prevalent within hospitals. Schimmel also found that 20 percent of patients investigated experienced deleterious complications associated with medical care. The incidence of life-threatening iatrogenic complications was approximately 5 percent of the total hospital population. The average duration of hospitalization for those who suffered iatrogenic effects was 28.7 days as compared to 11.4 days for unaffected patients. Whether the iatrogenic disease led to increased hospitalization or the prolonged hospitalization itself led to the iatrogenic complications is unclear, but most agree that the longer a person is hospitalized the more likely an iatrogenic incident will occur. Other researchers have found that once a patient has had one iatrogenic incident, the likelihood of having another is greatly increased. For example, in two studies approximately 30 percent of patients who were admitted to hospitals for adverse drug reactions experienced a second adverse event. Every test and procedure carries a definite risk. When tubes, or catheters, are inserted into veins, arteries or organs, there are definable hazards. A person may bleed excessively, develop an infection or have an organ injured. These complications require treatments that in turn carry their own risks.

The current state of excessive usage of drugs, diagnostic tests and procedures is due to many interacting factors: technological advancement; commercial interests; unrealistic patient expectations; legal concerns; financial solvency of medical institutions; and reimbursement procedures for health professionals.

The tendency to use the most recently developed medicines, even though their initial and long-term effects are not fully understood, obviously benefits the pharmaceutical industry. A new drug with a patent yields profits. The pharmaceutical industry is indeed interested in the well-being of people and the betterment of health. However, in the process of marketing a new drug, financial considerations often outweigh a cautious approach to therapeutic claims and a balanced appraisal of adverse effects. Moreover, physicians have not proven to be a major force against the appearance of such products, whose safety has not been fully established. Doctors perpetuate the introduction of new drugs by prescribing these agents and thus they provide consumers for the pharmaceutical companies. Gwynne has commented: "Deliberate or unconscious influence exerted by manufacturers to sell new products ... tend[s] to give undue emphasis to therapeutic advantages and commercial interests when the question of side effects is raised." In discussing science, Schiller, the eighteenth-century German poet, said, *"Einem ist sie die hohe, die himmlische Göttinn, dem andern/Eine tüchtige Kuh, die ihn mit Butter versorgt."* (For some it is the high, heavenly goddess, for others, a good cow to be milked.)

The rapidly expanding pharmaceutical industry, through use of 'its testing procedures, has been largely responsible for fostering the attitude of ridicule and disdain for the placebo effect. As discussed in chapter 4, if a new potentially active drug and an inert tablet were found to be equally efficacious, both were discarded. The placebo effect, or the effect of nonspecific factors of treatment, was not studied further because there was no profit in it. Yet, is not the positive placebo effect more desirable than a drug with side effects? Indeed, if the effects of a drug and those of nonspecific treatment factors are similar, why risk the toxicity of the drug?

All drugs have the potential for adverse effects. Some teachers of pharmacology have even stated that "all drugs are poisons." Drugs often work by altering the biochemistry of the body. When a biochemical system is diseased, this alteration is desirable. The benefits of the drug outweigh its risks, especially when no other options are available.

A conservative approach in medicine is safer for the patient since fewer tests and procedures are employed initially. If symptoms persist, additional tests and procedures should then be performed. Little will be lost by waiting. However, a conservative approach to medicine is difficult to maintain in our present society. When faced with legal action for not having made a rapid diagnosis, a physician may have difficulty defending this conservative position. The physician is made to appear negligent and behind the times even though the vast majority of his patients have benefited from this approach. As a result of these legal actions, "defensive medicine" is being practiced. Defensive medicine involves the ordering of a multitude of tests, regardless of their medical necessity or expense. Therefore, if a malpractice suit is filed, the physician cannot be accused of failure to obtain all "relevant" diagnostic information. Defensive medicine is a poor practice of medicine, as it is excessively expensive and invites iatrogenic disease. Thus the legal profession, due to its own lucrative role in malpractice suits, helps to perpetuate this vicious cycle. Defensive medicine is also encouraged by the financial interests of physicians, since third-party payments made to doctors by Blue Cross/Blue Shield and other insurance companies are often based upon the number of diagnostic or therapeutic procedures and tests performed.

Defensive medicine is also in the interest of many hospital administrators who are concerned with a hospital's solvency. The tests and procedures pay for the equipment bought to perform these tests. Ultimately, the tests and procedures are a source of income to the hospital and the physicians. Yet one cannot accuse hospital administrators since they have their defined priorities.

Another, much more insidious type of iatrogenic disease may be caused by people's excessive concern with health. This concern is fostered by a well meaning medical profession, by commercial interests or by both. High blood pressure, or hypertension, is a good example of how preoccupation with health may lead to disease.

Hypertension is a disease of excessive blood pressure within the arteries, and it is of unknown cause in the vast majority of cases. A person afflicted with hypertension usually has no symptoms for many years. Yet high blood pressure leads to an increased rate of hardening of the arteries or arteriosclerosis. Arteriosclerosis involves the deposition of fats, blood clots and calcium within the walls of arteries. It may lead to cerebral vascular accidents, commonly called strokes or shocks; myocardial infarctions, also called heart attacks or coronaries; or death of kidney cells. If hypertension is detected early enough, appropriate drug therapy can lower blood pressure and prevent these severe consequences. Arteriosclerotic disease affecting the heart, brain and kidney is the major cause of death in the United States today. Since hypertension can be treated, and these diseases prevented or delayed, extensive hypertension-detection campaigns have been initiated. These programs are certainly worthwhile if verifiable hypertension is discovered. However, the detection programs may be counterproductive.

A growing body of evidence supports the fact that emotional, or psychological, elements are important in the development of hypertension. If you are in a stressful situation, one which is emotionally disturbing or requires behavioral adjustment, an innate bodily response, the "fight or flight" response, is elicited. The fight or flight response is characterized by increased blood pressure, heart rate, rate of breathing, metabolism and blood flow to the muscles. All these physiological changes, it is believed, prepare you for running or fighting and hence the name, the fight or flight response. Repeated elicitation of the fight or flight response may lead from transient to permanent elevations of blood pressure. Hypertension is then present.

If emotional factors lead to hypertension, may some of our detection campaigns start a course of events which result in iatrogenic hypertension? Blood pressure fluctuates greatly throughout the day. Blood pressure is usually elevated in emotionally charged or stressful situations, such as during an argument. Only when it is consistently high should hypertension be diagnosed. Therefore, when blood pressure is measured in unsettling environments, for example, in airports, city plazas, supermarkets and busy drugstores, it might be higher than normal, but not truly indicative of hypertension.

There has been a recent proliferation of commercial devices which measure blood pressure automatically in many such public places. People are instructed to sit down in a chair, insert their arms in a blood-pressure cuff, put several coins into the device and watch the numbers appear on a screen in front of them. The numbers represent their blood pressure. If their blood pressure is recorded as being in the high range, people are instructed to consult with a doctor. Not only might the stressful environment contribute to a higher than normal blood pressure reading, but also these devices are generally unreliable. The unreliability is compounded by people who do not use them properly. For example, many do not remove clothing from their arms. The clothing impairs the already limited reliability of the machine.

Automatic machines and their improper use are not the only source of unrepresentative blood pressures. People have been educated about the grave results of undetected hypertension. The disease has been referred to as the "silent killer" and "internal time-bomb." Because of this widespread knowledge, many people become excessively anxious when their blood pressure is being measured. Once again, the anxiety may elevate blood pressure and hypertension may be misdiagnosed. I recently spoke to a person involved in a high blood pressure-detection campaign in a drugstore. I asked him whether he had detected many cases of high blood pressure. He said that, at first, he had been relatively unsuccessful, but had subsequently learned to measure blood pressure in a manner that greatly increased the number of cases. Originally he had simply measured blood pressure by inflating and deflating the cuff in the standard fashion, without making any comments. However, when he altered this procedure by looking concerned and muttering "Oh-oh," after the first measurement, a second measurement detected a very high incidence of hypertension in these subjects! He was thus able to refer many more people to physicians.

When a physician is consulted, the person knowing the dangers of high blood pressure might again be anxious. Another higher than normal blood pressure for that individual is recorded. In this way, a vicious cycle is started which ultimately results in the drug therapy of a disease which might not even be present.

Further education about the dangers of high blood pressure, as well as repeated measurements of blood pressure, may lead to the diagnosis of high blood pressure. Dr. William S. Aronow, Dr. William H. Allen, Dr. Dominic De Cristofaro and Ms. Suzanne Ungermann of the University of California at Irvine and Los Angeles analyzed the presence of coronary risk factors in people with no history of coronary heart disease. They measured the major risk factors of this disease (blood pressure, cholesterol levels in the blood serum, tobacco-smoking habits, obesity and tendency toward diabetes) in 2524 adults. After the first set of measurements, the subjects were divided into two groups. The first 1250 people who volunteered participated in an educational program concerning coronary risk factors. They were sent four separate mailings and were also invited to attend four evening lectures concerned with the reduction of these risk factors. During the lectures, the participants were divided into groups in which their individual questions were answered. The second group of subjects received no such educational interventions.

Ten to eleven months after the first set of measurements, all the participants were invited to be remeasured. Although some did not respond to the invitation, a sufficient number, 1817, returned. Comparisons were made between the group who underwent the educational program and those who did not. There were significantly increased blood pressures recorded during the second set of measurements in the group that participated in the educational program. The number of such subjects with elevated blood pressure was more than five times greater than that during the initial evaluation. Did the educational program lead to an increased awareness of the dangers of high blood pressure, and thus to increased anxiety and elevated blood pressures?

In previous years, the syndrome of transient anxiety-related hypertension leading to the erroneous diagnosis of "true" hypertension was seen primarily in medical students, due to their understanding of the consequences of high blood pressure. As the knowledge of the danger of high blood pressure has become more widespread, this syndrome is occurring more frequently in our informed population. High blood pressure is being recorded during many pre-employment examinations. People are often anxious during these examinations because of their concern for employment and their knowledge that an increased blood pressure might prevent them from being hired. If refused a job due to such "high blood pressure," subsequent pressures are also likely to be elevated.

Initial blood pressures should be measured in the relatively calm, standardized conditions of a physician's office. Health education strategies that scare people may well be counterproductive. We have created an iatrogenic disease caused by the circumstances under which the diagnosis was made and its interpretation explained. This iatrogenic disease has the potential of being complicated further since the prescribed drugs may have adverse side effects. If high blood pressure is truly present, there is no question that the risk of the adverse drug reactions is far outweighed by the benefits of the antihypertensive drugs. However, the correct diagnosis must be established before such therapy is initiated.

Generally, when you feel well, you are well. You should not seek excessive reassurance, such as repeated blood pressure recordings, when there are no medical complaints. You should not allow unwarranted worries about health to develop. The worries themselves may create a disease.

DESCRIPTIONS OF the sensation of pain have been recorded since man's earliest writings. By tracing the history of pain, comparisons of the practice of medicine throughout the ages are possible, since physicians or healers have always been called upon to alleviate pain. A discussion of pain also demonstrates how modern medicine, although capable of relieving pain as never before, is often unable to help many who suffer from this sensation. A combination of age-old techniques with our modern medical technology has not been successfully achieved. This is due, in part, to neglect of the principles of Behavioral Medicine. We have disregarded the nonspecific elements of treatment which lead to a positive placebo effect. Our inability to deal with pain has created problems because our current attitudes disregard a proper assessment of the risk versus benefit ratio. Pain is an example of how the mind and the body interact in an inseparable fashion. The sensation of pain represents a complex interaction of physiological and psychological factors.

Almost all regions of the body are supplied with specific nerve fibers that may be compared to telephone wires. These nerves transmit messages, or impulses, of "pain." When injury, disease and other factors trigger the endings of these special nerve fibers, messages are carried to the spinal cord and areas of the midbrain. The message of pain is "interpreted" first at the spinal cord and at these brain regions. The messages may result in a direct reflex such as the immediate withdrawal of a portion of the body from an injurious situation [see Figure 9]. The reflex withdrawal of a hand from a very hot object, which occurs without conscious perception of the immediate message, is an example. The reflex may be compared to a prerecorded message transmitted back along the telephone wire to the caller. However, when the majority of painful sensations reach the level of the spinal cord and midbrain, they are modified before they are interpreted and before a response is generated. The modification is achieved by nerve impulses arising within the spinal cord itself and by other impulses from the brain to the area of the spinal cord where the impulses entered. The central nervous system acts like a switchboard, letting some messages go through, modifying others and blocking yet others. The switchboard is programmed, in part, by "higher centers" of the nervous system, which are other areas of the brain. In these areas, both physio-

117

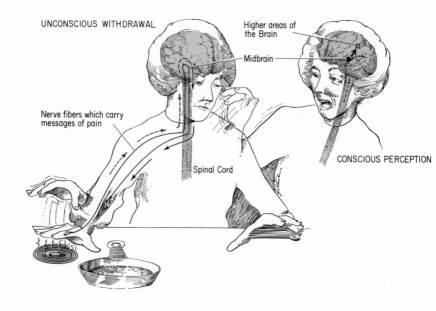

FIGURE 9   Pain Sensation with Reflex Withdrawal
Followed by Awareness.

Messages of pain are transmitted from the burned hand along
specific nerve fibers to the spinal cord and to areas of the
midbrain. The painful impulses of the injury first lead to
the unconscious reflex withdrawal of the hand. This reflex
withdrawal occurs without awareness. The reflex is controlled
by "lower" centers of the central nervous system. Fractions
of a second later, the painful messages are transmitted to
higher areas of the brain. The impulses are then interpreted
as being painful, the person recognizes pain, and consciously
reacts.

118

logical mechanisms and psychological interpretations of pain are integrated [see Figure 9]. The higher centers of the nervous system are the anatomical regions of the brain which are associated with consciousness. To a large extent, these centers determine which messages of pain are ultimately transmitted to consciousness. *Psychological factors affect the conscious perception of, and sensitivity to, pain.*

Attitude is one such psychological factor which may influence one's reaction to pain. To illustrate this, we may assess the experience of pain in various cultural groups. Dr. Mark Zborowski reported in 1952 the differences in attitudes toward, and reactions to, pain among "Old American," Jewish and Italian patients. The project was conducted at the Kingsbridge Veterans Hospital in New York. It consisted of interviews with patients of the selected ethnic groups, observations of their behavior when in pain and discussions about the individual patients with medical personnel who were present during the patients' painful experiences. Zborowski found that members of the Italian and Jewish cultures were highly sensitive to pain and very emotional in their responses to it. However, their underlying attitudes toward pain were quite different. Italian patients were concerned with immediate pain relief, whereas patients of Jewish origin were more concerned with the implications of pain as related to their health and to the future welfare of their families. "Old American" individuals, defined as white, native born, usually Protestant, and whose grandparents at least were born in the United States, were much less verbal about pain and had great confidence in the ability of their doctors to alleviate it. This investigation was of a qualitative nature however, and the information collected did not lend itself to quantitative analysis.

More recently, Dr. Richard A. Sternbach and Bernard Tursky of Harvard Medical School quantified differences in attitudes toward pain among these same ethnic groups and also for individuals of Irish extraction. Housewives who were members of the selected ethnic groups volunteered to participate in this study, in which electrical stimuli were administered. Data were collected regarding the intensity of electrical stimulation that could be tolerated by the subjects, the ability to discriminate differences in stimulus intensity and also the subjects' physiological responses to repeated electrical stimulation. In this investigation cultural differences in attitudes toward pain were similar to those witnessed by Zborowski. Further, Irish people inhibited expression of suffering and masked their concern for the implications of the pain.

PHANTOM PAIN

Another interesting phenomenon which demonstrates the importance of interpretative aspects of pain is the "phantom pain" syndrome. Most patients who undergo an amputation continue to have an "awareness" of their amputated part following surgery. Although this awareness occurs most often with the loss of an arm or leg, it may also be present after a nose, ear or other part of the body is lost. The famous French military surgeon, Ambroise Paré, described this phenomenon in 1551, but the term "phantom limb" was not introduced until the 1870s, by Dr. Silas Wier Mitchell, an American neurologist. Not only are patients aware of an amputated portion of their bodies, but some also experience pain in this "phantom" part. The perception and intensity of phantom pain fluctuates considerably among individuals and may also vary from day to day in the same person. The pain may be worsened by emotional stress and fatigue.

In one case of phantom pain, a 51-year-old man who had experienced mild sensations in his amputated arm for almost twenty years developed the symptom of angina pectoris. Angina pectoris is the specific pain which is experienced when the heart muscle does not receive sufficient oxygen. Most often this pain is felt in the front portion of the chest, and occasionally the pain is sensed in the arms, neck and jaw. In this patient the pain of his angina pectoris radiated to his phantom limb.

Several theories attempt to explain the phenomenon of phantom pain. One theory is that continual irritation of the nerves at the site of the amputation is interpreted by the central nervous system as pain in the absent limb. Another theory, according to the neurosurgeon Dr. Bernard E. Finneson, is based upon the concept that a person unconsciously attempts to maintain an intact body image even after loss of a body part. It is thought that body image begins to develop in infancy. As a child gains increasing awareness of his or her body, these various impressions contribute to a fixed body image which is resistant to change. Others also feel that the persistence of a total body image is the critical aspect of the phantom pain phenomenon. Adults who have had an amputation in infancy, or who lack a limb due to a congenital defect, do not experience phantom pain. The loss of the limb occurred prior to the establishment of a fixed body image. It has been observed that social outcasts living in New York City's Bowery district infrequently develop phantom symptoms. This has been attributed to a loss of body image, due to their unfortunate lives. The phantom pain phenomenon supports the concept that the presence or absence of pain is partly dependent upon psychological considerations.

PAIN RELIEF

There are both biological and psychological interpretative aspects of pain and these cannot be separated. *However, the usual approach of modern medical science to the treatment of pain consists of altering the biological pathways without regard to the regulating psychological aspects.* This therapeutic approach has been very successful in the alleviation of pain that was previously untreatable. Surgery without pain was not possible, and extensive surgical incisions and procedures could be performed only when patients were tied or held down. Although anesthetic agents and procedures, those substances or techniques which produce insensibility to pain and other sensations, had been used since antiquity, their efficacy was limited. Dr. Peter J. Cohen of the University of Colorado and Dr. Robert D. Dripps of the University of Pennsylvania note that the ancient Chinese employed hashish to induce anesthesia. Some Roman physicians used mandragora, an extract of mandrake roots that contained belladonna, to produce unconsciousness. The Assyrians rendered children undergoing circumcision insensible to pain by partial strangulation that resulted in temporary unconsciousness. Brain concussions were another method by which people were made unconscious. Some concussions were caused by placing a wooden bowl upon the head of a patient and striking it forcefully with a blunt object. Opium and alcoholic beverages were most often used, but their anesthetic effect was not sufficient to eliminate pain. In 1800 Sir Humphry Davy, an English chemist, observed that nitrous oxide, "laughing gas," had the ability to destroy pain, and in 1818 Michael Faraday, an English physicist and chemist, reported the anesthetic effects of ether. However, Dr. Daniel De Moulin, formerly affiliated with the Johns Hopkins Institute of the History of Medicine, suggests that prior to the 1840s, the complete absence of pain was deemed unrealistic. It is therefore not surprising that the medical profession considered the findings of Davy and Faraday unbelievable or a hoax.

In 1846, when William T. G. Morton, a Boston dentist, who was at the time a second-year Harvard Medical School student, gained permission to carry out a public demonstration of the effectiveness of ether during a surgical operation, his audience was skeptical. The surgeon, Dr. John C. Warren of Massachusetts General Hospital, was astonished that the patient experienced no pain during the operation and that the strong men usually required to hold down patients were not needed. After this dramatic, first demonstration of surgery without pain, Dr. Warren turned to his astounded audience and said, "Gentlemen, this is no humbug."

The general anesthetic agents, such as ether, act upon the central nervous system to produce insensibility to pain and other sensations [see Figure 10]. The exact mechanism of this action is still not fully understood. Other anesthetic agents which render a patient insensible to feeling in a specific area of the body also became available. The "local anesthetics," such as lidocaine, block or impair the transmission of messages along the nerve fibers. Hence, the messages of pain never reach the spinal cord [see Figure 11]. Other pain messages may be interrupted at the spinal cord itself by use of "spinal anesthesia" [see Figure 12]. Pain messages therefore do not reach the higher centers which are concerned with consciousness. In 1884 a young physician, Dr. Sigmund Freud, the

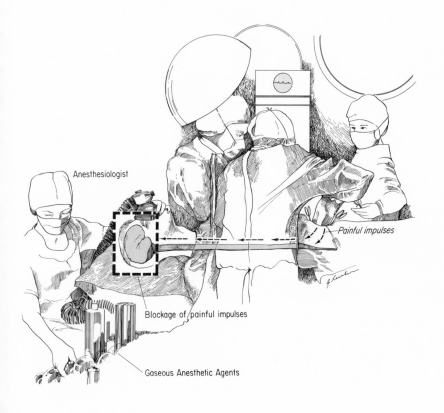

Anesthesiologist

Painful impulses

Blockage of painful impulses

Gaseous Anesthetic Agents

FIGURE 10   GENERAL ANESTHESIA.

An anesthesiologist administers a gaseous anesthetic agent, such as ether, to a patient undergoing surgery. The painful impulses of the surgery, indicated by the arrows, do not reach the patient's consciousness. These impulses are "blocked" within the brain. The region of "blockage" is indicated by the rectangle composed of an interrupted line.

125

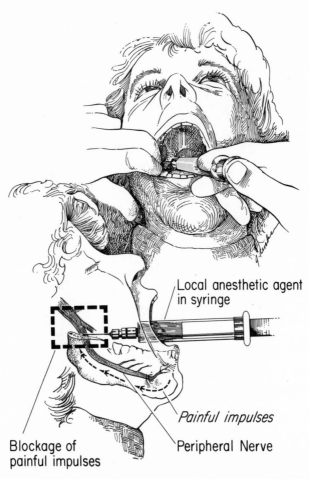

Local anesthetic agent
in syringe

Painful impulses

Peripheral Nerve

Blockage of
painful impulses

FIGURE 11 LOCAL ANESTHESIA IN A PERIPHERAL NERVE.

A dentist injects a local anesthetic agent such as lidocaine in the area of a nerve. The painful impulses, indicated by the arrows, from the area of the tooth and mouth are blocked in this peripheral nerve. These impulses therefore do not reach the higher areas of the central nervous system. The patient is unaware of pain. The rectangle made of an interrupted line indicates this peripheral region of blockage.

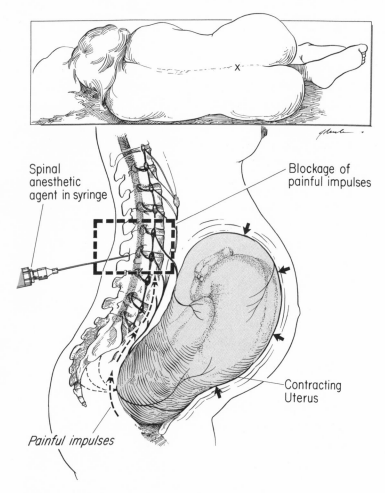

FIGURE 12   SPINAL ANESTHESIA.

An anesthesiologist injects an anesthetic agent into a region
of the spinal cord in a pregnant woman in labor. The painful
impulses, indicated by the broken arrows, of the woman's
contracting uterus do not reach consciousness since they are
blocked at the level of the spinal cord. The area of blockage
is indicated by the rectangle made of an interrupted line.

127

father of psychoanalysis, made the firs[t]
of the physiological effects of cocai[ne] [as an]
anesthetic. Freud used cocaine to [cure his]
colleagues from the use of morp[hine. He]
was successful in this attempt, he allegedly [became]
the first reported cocaine addict of modern times. Dr.
Karl Köller, another Viennese physician of the late
nineteenth century, recognized the anesthetic properties of cocaine, which were described by Freud, and
used cocaine as a local anesthetic in the practice of
ophthalmology. Shortly thereafter, local anesthesia
was introduced into the fields of dentistry and
surgery.

We have made major advances in pain relief. However, we still do not totally understand pain mechanisms. The current concept of the physiology of
pain, which I previously described in terms of a telephone switchboard, was formulated by Drs. Ronald
Melzack of McGill University, Montreal, Canada,
and Patrick D. Wall of Massachusetts Institute of
Technology, and is called the "gate control theory."
Although it does not fully explain all phenomena related to pain or pain relief, it is a workable hypothesis. The use of acupuncture for the relief of
pain can be understood within the framework of this
hypothesis. Acupuncture probably acts to impair the
transmission of pain impulses to the brain, either by
altering the capacity of the nerves which carry messages to the central nervous system or by changing
the programming of the central nervous system itself.
The transmission of impulses along nerve fibers is

is it ever in danger. Only
his prey, he shoots forth
like so many darts, and
the fish through the wat[er]
defend itself nor escape,
chains and frozen up.

One of the first descripti[on]
electricity is attributed t[o]
pharmacist and physician,

For any type of gout a
when the pain begins, be
patient must stand on a
sea and he should stay lik[e]
and leg up to the knee
present pain and prevent[s]
it has not already arisen
freedman of Tiberius, was

Claudius Galen, the ren[owned]
physician, found that appli[ed]
to the head of a patient
headache was efficacious
ache even if it is chronic
away and remedied f[or]
placed on the s[pot]
ceases . . . M[any]
kind

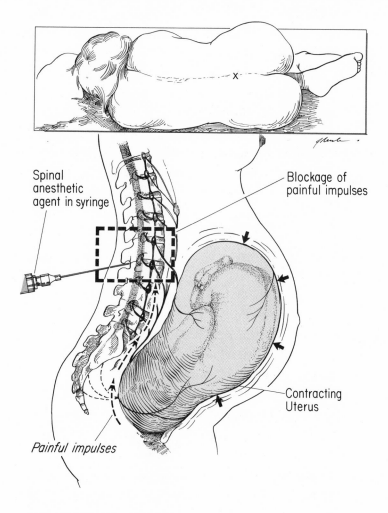

Spinal anesthetic agent in syringe

Blockage of painful impulses

Contracting Uterus

Painful impulses

FIGURE 12   SPINAL ANESTHESIA.

An anesthesiologist injects an anesthetic agent into a region of the spinal cord in a pregnant woman in labor. The painful impulses, indicated by the broken arrows, of the woman's contracting uterus do not reach consciousness since they are blocked at the level of the spinal cord. The area of blockage is indicated by the rectangle made of an interrupted line.

127

father of psychoanalysis, made the first detailed study of the physiological effects of cocaine, another local anesthetic. Freud used cocaine to wean one of his colleagues from the use of morphine. Although he was successful in this attempt, he allegedly produced the first reported cocaine addict of modern times. Dr. Karl Köller, another Viennese physician of the late nineteenth century, recognized the anesthetic properties of cocaine, which were described by Freud, and used cocaine as a local anesthetic in the practice of ophthalmology. Shortly thereafter, local anesthesia was introduced into the fields of dentistry and surgery.

We have made major advances in pain relief. However, we still do not totally understand pain mechanisms. The current concept of the physiology of pain, which I previously described in terms of a telephone switchboard, was formulated by Drs. Ronald Melzack of McGill University, Montreal, Canada, and Patrick D. Wall of Massachusetts Institute of Technology, and is called the "gate control theory." Although it does not fully explain all phenomena related to pain or pain relief, it is a workable hypothesis. The use of acupuncture for the relief of pain can be understood within the framework of this hypothesis. Acupuncture probably acts to impair the transmission of pain impulses to the brain, either by altering the capacity of the nerves which carry messages to the central nervous system or by changing the programming of the central nervous system itself. The transmission of impulses along nerve fibers is analogous to the transmission of electrical impulses along a wire.

It is also possible to interrupt transmission of nerve impulses through the use of externally applied electrical currents to change the properties of the nerve fiber. In fact, electrical currents have been used for centuries in the amelioration of pain. Dr. Peter Kellaway of McGill University, Montreal, Canada and Dr. Dennis Stillings, Director of the Museum of Electricity in Life at Medtronic in Minneapolis, Minnesota, each discuss the medical use of electricity in previous ages. The ancient source of the electrical current was the electrical discharge of certain types of fish, including the eel and torpedo fish. Astute observers recognized that electricity, which was not then defined, had the ability to be conducted through water. Plutarch, the first/second-century Greek biographer and philosopher, described this electrical property:

> You know yourself the property of the torpedo or cramp fish, which not only benumbs all those that touch it, but also strikes a numbness through the very net into the hands of them that go about to take it. And some that have had greater experience of this fish report that if it happens to fall alive upon the land, they that pour water upon it shall presently perceive a numbness seizing upon their hands and stupefying their feelings, *through the water affected with the quality of the fish.* And therefore having an innate sense of this faculty, it never takes any resistance against any thing nor

is it ever in danger. Only swimming circularly about his prey, he *shoots forth the effluviums of his nature* like so many darts, and *first infects the water, then the fish through the water* which is neither able to defend itself nor escape, being (as it were) held in chains and frozen up.

One of the first descriptions of the therapeutic use of electricity is attributed to the first-century Roman pharmacist and physician, Scribonius:

For any type of gout a live black torpedo should, when the pain begins, be placed under the feet. The patient must stand on a moist shore washed by the sea and he should stay like this until his whole foot and leg up to the knee is numb. This takes away present pain and prevents pain from coming on if it has not already arisen. In this way Anteros, a freedman of Tiberius, was cured.

Claudius Galen, the renowned first-century Greek physician, found that application of a live torpedo fish to the head of a patient who was suffering from headache was efficacious in relieving pain: "Headache even if it is chronic and unbearable is taken away and remedied forever by a live black torpedo placed on the spot which is in pain, until the pain ceases ... Moreover several torpedoes of the same kind should be prepared because the cure, that is, the torpor which is a sign of betterment, is sometimes effective only after two or three."

The use of the torpedo fish persisted throughout the Middle Ages, although some physicians eliminated the effective but discomforting element of the therapy, the electrical current, by first killing the fish. Alexander of Tralles, a Byzantine physician, wrote in the sixth century:

> Throw a live torpedo fish [Torpedo galvanii] into a copper container, put in some oil, place it all in a pot with water, so that the oil does not burn or evaporate. Add to this the narcissus plant [Narcissus, L.], picked during the last quarter of the moon. Once mixed with the animal, cook it all until it is completely dissolved and the bones are bare. Then merely extract the rest of the oil carefully from the pot of water. All these operations will take place in the period of the waning moon. Then use the oil to anoint the patient three times a day. If he is suffering, at the moment, from his joints, this will cure it, if he does not feel anything, this will protect him from all future pain. One should practice these anointings for three days, the moon being completely at its wane, because at another time, they will not succeed.

If this therapy was efficacious, it was most likely due to a positive placebo effect.

In Europe the application of artificially generated electrical currents as therapy for pain largely replaced the use of the electric fish by the middle of the eighteenth century. The invention of the Leyden jar in 1745 enabled the storage of a generated electrical charge. This charge could be of greater intensity than that produced by an electric fish, and also it could be delivered when desired by the physician and patient. John Wesley, the eighteenth-century English theologian and physician, employed "electrifying" in the treatment of most aches and pains. He described: "*Mary Butler*, aged 86, living in *Eagle-street, Redlion square*, having been afflicted with the *Sciatica* for more than twenty Years, was last Month electrified ten or twelve Times, and has been easy ever since," and also "*Mr. Joshua W—* of *Pershore*, [who] was troubled for seven or eight Years with a Pain in his second Toe. Tho' nothing was to be seen, it was as tender as a Boil, and the Pain was so great, particularly in walking, that he at length determined to have it cut off. By drawing Sparks he was cured in an Hour."

Electrical currents, now generated by a variety of devices, are still being used for different types of pain. The results are promising but inconclusive. A patient's expectation of obtaining relief from pain may contribute to the effectiveness of the electrical treatment. The intrinsic effects of the electrical current have not been separated from those nonspecific elements of a positive placebo effect.

Recently a new focus has emerged in pain research which is concerned with the alteration of pain perceptions by chemical substances produced within the brain itself. There is considerable evidence that certain parts of the midbrain of man and other animals participate in the process of analgesia, or insensibility only to pain, through the secretion of the chemicals, endorphins and enkephalins. The chemical structure of the endorphins and enkephalins appears to be very similar to that of morphine and its derivatives.

132

Like morphine, the pain-alleviating effects of these newly discovered compounds can be completely reversed by the drug naloxone. These findings are exciting, as they suggest that humans have a "natural" morphine-like substance that can produce analgesia. These natural compounds released within the brain may play a major role in modifying sensitivity to pain. The positive placebo effect, which affords pain relief, may be related to their secretion.

Through continued research, we are gaining a better understanding of pain. Today we are able to alleviate most types of pain through the use of pharmacological anesthetic agents. However, pain is still the most common complaint that patients present to doctors. Have we lost something from older medical practices which might be incorporated into modern medicine? How was pain managed in other generations who lived prior to the advent of anesthesia? Physicians for centuries have described the worth of nonspecific therapeutic approaches which utilized the principles of a positive placebo effect. Avicenna, an Arab physician and philosopher of the eleventh century, knew that diversion, for example, pleasant soothing songs, could lessen pain.* St. Thomas Aquinas, the thirteenth-century philosopher and theologian, wrote that pain could be relieved by meditating upon divine matters. Galen insisted that a physician should take into account the fears of the patient because the fears influence the reaction of the

---

* Significant portions of this discussion are derived from the work of Dr. Daniel De Moulin.

patient. Seneca, a Roman philosopher and writer who lived at the time of Christ, was well aware that emotional factors and a patient's attitude affect the experience of pain. He wrote: "young soldiers, although only slightly wounded, cry and fear the hand of the surgeons even more than the sword of the enemy, ... [whereas] veterans, even if they are pierced through, patiently and without complaint endure that their body, as if it were someone else's, is cleaned from dirt." Dr. Baron Guillaume Dupuytren, a French eighteenth/nineteenth-century surgeon, compared the reactions of different people to the same surgical procedure:

> What a difference there is in the morale of those we treat in civil hospitals and those hit by murderous fire on the field of battle! The military man is accustomed to forgetfulness of self and familiar with the prospect of mutilation. He considers himself happy if he saves his life yet loses an extremity. And, as long as he is assured of security ... he faces with courage, even joy, the scalpel of the surgeon. But look at the unfortunate laborer, the farmer, or the artisan, whose work is the only resource of a large family. He is obsessed by fear; misery awaits him. His is a profound sorrow, a dark hopelessness.

These accounts demonstrate that the sensation of pain can be lessened by changing one's attitude toward pain, by diversion or by altering expectations.

Even after the advent of anesthesia, similar differences in reaction to pain have been described. Beecher investigated the frequency of pain severe enough to require medications in 150 male civilian patients undergoing surgery. He contrasted these findings with similar data he had obtained from 150 wounded soldiers on the Anzio Beachhead in World War II. Although the two groups were studied at different periods of time, efforts were made to match the groups with respect to the part of the body involved, age and previous medical history. The soldiers had very extensive wounds but were mentally alert and were capable of being questioned. Only 32 percent said that the pain was severe enough to warrant asking for medication. In contrast, 83 percent of the civilians requested medication. Beecher concluded, in part, that "the intensity of suffering is largely determined by what pain means to the patient."

We have created an increased psychological awareness of pain. In our current society pain is poorly tolerated. De Moulin cites the Dutch professor, F. J. J. Buytendijk:

> Modern man takes offense at many things that used to be accepted with resignation. He takes offense at growing old, at a long sick-bed, frequently even at death, but certainly at pain. Its occurrence is inacceptable. The demand to do away with pain becomes progressively stronger, as every doctor, dentist, surgeon or obstetrician knows from daily experience.

De Moulin traces pain through history and concludes that pain was experienced physiologically as acutely in the past as it is today. Since there is no reason to assume that the human nervous system has significantly changed in the past several thousand years, his conclusion is not surprising. He points out that pain was experienced in every age of Western man from Homer to the present day and that "we have to attribute the rapidly dwindling readiness to accept pain to a change in our mental attitude." The inability to accept pain may be traced to the mind-body separation of Descartes. Since pain is of the body and the body may be modified, there is little reason to subject the mind to pain. Our current medical approaches that deal with the sensation of pain reinforce this mind-body separation. People believe that a pain-relieving medication should be able to eliminate bodily pain regardless of what the mind perceives.

Leonato, in Shakespeare's *Much Ado About Nothing*, observed: "For there was never yet philosopher/ That could endure the toothache patiently..." The anesthetic agents have even been called a blessing to mankind. However, perhaps because of our very successes, we have come to believe that any pain is intolerable and that we should always seek relief from it.

COMMERCIAL INTEREST IN PAIN

Commercial interests have exploited this attitude of intolerance to pain and the unrealistic expectation that life without the sensation of pain is possible. We are deluged by over-the-counter remedies for pain relief. Advertisements appear on television, on the radio and in the other news media. These advertisements use allegedly scientific facts, silly animated diagrams and personal testimonials regarding the superiority of one pain-relieving substance over another. Most of these analgesic agents contain aspirin as an active ingredient. The difference among these medications lies primarily in the amount of aspirin present.

The extensive advertising probably has created more pain than it has alleviated. It has made you aware of pain which might not otherwise have been perceived or which would have been disregarded. Commercialism has fostered the attitude that any pain is unacceptable and should be eradicated. The commercial interests have not fully weighed the relative risks of such advertising. Their motivation is primarily to sell drugs. The benefits of an exaggerated awareness of pain are essentially nonexistent. Have we not therefore allowed ourselves to believe that we are more ill than we truly are? We have been programmed into excessive reliance upon pain medications. I emphasize that you should not stop taking the medications which do alleviate your pain. I ask you to reassess your attitude toward pain. Then, along with your physician, determine whether the medications you are now taking are actually necessary. With your physician's reassurance and with your own understanding, perhaps you can begin decreasing the amount of this pain medication and become more reliant upon your inherent resources. You must remember that pain is determined to a large extent by the recognition and interpretation of it. Do not allow business interests to define your state of health by making you aware of the sensation of pain.

Like voodoo death, which was dependent upon one's belief in voodoo and could only be prevented by voodoo techniques, pain created by belief in its presence can be relieved only by an alteration of one's belief system. Pain has a psychological, interpretative as well as a biological aspect. The psychological component of your pain should be managed by changes in attitude, not with medications.

RESEARCH WHICH INTEGRATES both old and new concepts should be encouraged. There should also be extensive research on the healing practices of other cultures. *However, this research must be based upon the modern scientific principles which have proven so successful. Without adherence to the scientific approach, we could fall victim to the claims of charlatans preying upon our fears and anxieties concerning illness and mortality.* We should investigate medical problems as they affect the entire human being to understand better how the mind and the body interact.

Our laboratory has studied the physiology associated with meditative practices. These studies have led to the definition of an innate, physiological response, the "relaxation response." This research was interdisciplinary, encompassing studies of interaction between the mind (psychology and psychiatry) and the body (physiology and medicine). The integration of these research areas is compatible with Behavioral Medicine. The use of the relaxation response constitutes one therapeutic application of Behavioral Medicine.

The relaxation response is elicited through specific behavioral practices and techniques which have existed for centuries, including certain types of prayers, Eastern meditative techniques and Western relaxation techniques. These practices contain four basic components necessary to elicit the relaxation response. The components are: a comfortable position; a quiet environment; repetition of a prayer, word, sound or phrase; adoption of a passive attitude when other thoughts come into consciousness. The relaxation response, which is elicited by these specific behaviors, is the counterpart of the fight or flight response.

The fight or flight response, which was discussed in chapter 6, is a physiological response to stressful situations. Its repeated elicitation has been implicated in the development of stress-related diseases such as hypertension. The fight or flight response is characterized by increased activity of the sympathetic nervous system, that is, increased secretion of epinephrine (adrenaline) and norepinephrine (noradrenaline). On the other hand, the relaxation response is associated with decreased activity of this system. By reducing sympathetic nervous system activity, the relaxation response is therapeutically useful in stress-related diseases and may also be useful in their prevention. Behavioral approaches, such as elicitation of the relaxation response, in conjunction with conventional medical practices would be a most effective therapy for stress-related illnesses.

Hypertension, premature ventricular contractions (a type of irregular heartbeat), symptoms associated with anxiety and tension headaches are excellent examples of conditions related to stress and do not conform to the separation of the mind from the body. All are directly related to sympathetic nervous system activity and sympathetic nervous system activity is, in turn, usually related to an individual's state of mind. When you are excited, there is increased sympathetic nervous system activity. There are corresponding increases in blood pressure, in the tendency to experience anxiety and in the tendency to have irregular heartbeats. It is not surprising, therefore, that recent research has indicated the usefulness of the relaxation response in the therapy of these conditions. This behavioral approach is effective in states in which increased activity of the sympathetic nervous system is undesirable.

Occasional premature ventricular contractions are not dangerous in a healthy individual and are not predictive of future disease. However, in a patient suffering from blockage of the blood vessels which supply the heart muscle with nutrients, premature ventricular contractions may trigger life-threatening heart rhythms, such as ventricular tachycardia and ventricular fibrillation. It is advisable therefore to treat premature ventricular contractions in patients with coronary artery disease. Dr. Sidney Alexander of Boston's Lahey Clinic Foundation, Dr. Charles L. Feldman of Worcester Polytechnic Institute and I investigated the effects of regular elicitation of the relaxation response on the frequency of premature ventricular contractions. Eleven patients who suffered from coronary artery disease were studied. Most had not responded to the medications usually prescribed for this irregular heart rhythm. Therefore they were not taking drugs which could influence the results of this investigation. All patients underwent forty-eight hours of continuous monitoring of their heartbeat while they performed their normal daily activities. Such monitoring is routinely possible due to the pioneering work of Dr. Norman J. Holter of Helena, Montana. A person can wear electrocardiographic devices during the day and carry a tape cassette which records the electrical component of every heartbeat. Initial "baseline" or control recordings were obtained during forty-eight hours of "Holter-monitoring." All patients were taught, in approximately five minutes, a technique to elicit the relaxation response. They were instructed to practice the technique ten to twenty minutes twice daily. Four weeks later, the patients returned for another forty-eight-hour session of Holter-monitoring. Comparisons were made between the number of premature ventricular contractions in the two forty-eight-hour sessions. Eight of the eleven patients decreased the frequency of these irregular heartbeats in the second forty-eight-hour period, after they had regularly elicited the relaxation response for four weeks.

Support for these findings has subsequently come from other laboratories. The report of Lown and his associates of the man who collapsed with ventricular fibrillation after rough-housing with his daughters was described in chapter 2. These investigators found that the elicitation of the relaxation response, through use of transcendental meditation, was effective in decreasing the frequency of premature ventricular contractions. Dr. Panos C. Voukydis and Dr. Stanley A. Forwand of Mt. Auburn Hospital in Cambridge, Massachusetts, have reported that the elicitation of the relaxation response was a beneficial therapy for dangerous electrical rhythms of the heart in seven patients. These abnormal rhythms were of the same nature as those described in chapter 2, rhythms which often preceded sudden death.

Dr. Ruanne K. Peters of the Harvard School of Public Health found that the regular elicitation of the relaxation response was beneficial in alleviating symptoms associated with anxiety. The results of this investigation were published in collaboration with me, Dr. Douglas Porter, and Dr. John M. Peters. The effects of daily "relaxation response breaks" were investigated in Wilmington, Massachusetts, at the corporate offices of Converse, a division of Eltra Corporation. One hundred and twenty individuals volunteered to participate in the study. After four weeks of baseline measurements, they were randomly divided into three groups. One group was taught to elicit the relaxation response and practiced the technique one to two times daily. A second group simply sat quietly using no relaxation technique. The third group, which served as a control group, did not alter their behavior. The participants in the group who regularly elicited the relaxation response had lower blood pressures, fewer "illness days," and enhanced work performance when compared with participants in the other groups. The group who regularly elicited the relaxation response also manifested fewer symptoms associated with anxiety—headache, nausea, rashes, diarrhea, mouth sores, difficulty getting to sleep, worrying, and nervous habits such as chewing pencils and biting fingernails. These symptoms related to anxiety were alleviated by use of a behavioral approach.

The beneficial changes resulting from elicitation of the relaxation response had previously been attributed to a positive placebo effect. Meditative prayer was thought to be useful in the therapy of a number of diseases, but the effects of prayer were felt to be nonspecific. Further interdisciplinary research on the placebo effect should yield more precise information. However, scientific experimental designs which are now widely accepted will have to be modified in order to study the placebo effect. These experimental designs evolved from investigations which tested the potency and effectiveness of new drugs. These designs were formulated to eliminate the placebo effect as a complicating feature.

How can an experiment adequately investigate the placebo effect when the current methodology controls for the placebo effect? We should adopt new designs which still meet rigorous scientific standards but allow the placebo effect to be studied. When a better understanding of the placebo effect is attained, we should be able to translate these nonspecific general effects into other definable, predictable and useful therapies. Age-old practices such as prayer should not be viewed mechanistically. Rather, if future investigations are successful, they will continue to reaffirm the value of these practices.

Other behavioral approaches are being reintroduced into the practice of modern medicine. The medical, spiritual and emotional needs of dying patients and their families have generally not been fulfilled. The terminally ill patient frequently experiences isolation and depersonalization. The isolation increases as death approaches. Dr. Elisabeth Kübler-Ross has written several books concerned with death and the process of dying. She emphasizes that the current depersonalized medical approaches should be replaced wtih meaningful doctor-patient relationships. Kübler-Ross believes that modern doctors deal with death less effectively because of the technology now available. Others, particularly English and Canadian health-care professionals working in "hospices" and "palliative care units," have successfully applied the principles of Behavioral Medicine to meet the needs of the dying patient and to improve the quality of remaining life.

St. Christopher's Hospice in London is a small institution for terminally ill patients. Its main goal is to meet both the needs of the patient and of the patient's family, whether these needs be medical, social, psychological or spiritual. Dr. Ciceley Saunders, Medical Director of the hospice, lists the basic principles of palliative care, including concern for the patient and family as a unit; effective home care; and an interdisciplinary team approach to individualized patient care.

The Palliative Care Unit at the Royal Victoria Hospital in Montreal also emphasizes the "multidimensional needs" of the patient. The interdisciplinary staff at this institution helps the patient to maintain "a positive outlook based on reality, confidence and trust . . ." The staff also assists the patient when he or she prefers to stay at home and encourages family members to participate in care. The environment of the unit is made more pleasant by not enforcing standard regulations, allowing children to visit and relatives to stay overnight. Routine measurements, such as blood pressure and temperature, are taken only if "directly related to the alleviation of problematic symptoms." The unit also offers support for the patient's family after the patient has died.

There continues to be a need for modern technology in the care of the terminally ill patient. However, traditional behavioral practices of attending to the emotional requirements of patients and their families must not be forgotten or neglected.

The positive placebo effect has been demonstrated

to be a valuable asset in the treatment of patients. Drs. Lawrence D. Egbert, George E. Battit, Claude E. Welch and Marshall K. Bartlett of Harvard Medical School reported the effectiveness of a behavioral approach which utilized the positive placebo effect in the management of pain after surgery. These investigators assigned patients who were scheduled for elective abdominal surgery to either a control group or a "special-care" group. The control group was comprised of thirty patients and there were twenty-seven patients in the special-care group. Prior to the operation, the anesthetist did not discuss postoperative pain with the patients in the control group; they received standard medical treatment. Each of the patients in the special-care group was told by the anesthetist, before the operation was performed, where they would experience pain, how long it would last and how severe it would be. These special-care patients were also reassured that pain was to be expected following abdominal surgery. The physiological basis of the pain was explained. These patients were advised that they could relieve most of their pain by conscious relaxation of the abdominal muscles. They were also shown how to move about more comfortably in bed by using an overhead bar. The special-care patients were instructed to ask for pain-relieving medications if they could not achieve a reasonable degree of comfort. The explanations were given by anesthetists "in a manner of enthusiasm and confidence."

The operations were performed by surgeons who

did not know which of their patients had been given this special attention. The patients in the special-care group were visited by anesthetists for several days after the surgery and were again reassured. The pain-alleviating drugs requested by the patients were ordered by resident physicians and administered by ward nurses. Both the physicians and nurses were unaware that the patients were being investigated. The amount of pain-alleviating medication required in the special-care group was half that required in the control group. The special-care patients were discharged from the hospital, on the average, 2.7 days sooner than the control patients. The length of hospitalization was determined by surgeons who were unaware of the care each patient had received. Realistic patient expectations, an enthusiastic and confident physician and a sound doctor-patient relationship are essential components of the positive placebo effect. In this investigation, these components were used effectively with surgical techniques to achieve better therapeutic results.

Behavioral approaches, such as use of the positive placebo effect and elicitation of the relaxation response, are safe and effective. The safety of these approaches should be contrasted with that of modern medicine, which often employs pharmaceutical agents. If behavioral and pharmaceutical approaches each have similar therapeutic advantages, the lesser risk of the behavioral methods greatly enhances their value. A combination of both approaches may well constitute optimal medical management.

9

A RETURN TO the "natural" state which existed prior to the introduction of modern medicine would be unacceptable. The standard of health of people living in previous ages was totally inferior to the standard of health we have in America today. The number of deaths at all ages of life was excessive. Childhood mortality was staggering; more than 50 percent of children died before reaching age 5. Individuals died or were crippled from polio (infantile paralysis). Those who survived through childhood often suffered from lifelong infirmities, such as clubfoot, dislocated hips and cleft palates, which are now medically correctable. Many congenital heart diseases that resulted in early death or lifelong disability are now curable by open-heart surgery. Smallpox scarred most faces. Few people had healthy teeth into adulthood. In the Middle Ages this health problem was so common that it was popular to wear pomanders, pungent-smelling sub-stances enclosed in a perforated container, around the neck to overpower the odor of decaying teeth.

Therefore, I am clearly not advocating that we return to this "natural" state. Rather, I am concerned with problems which are unique to modern medicine. Specialization has strengthened the belief that the mind and the body can and should be separate. Problems have originated from the disdain for the placebo effect. Iatrogenesis has resulted directly from medical advances and from the commercialization of people's medical needs. Problems have occurred because of our propensity to adopt, without question, the "newest" approaches even though their validity remains to be established. We do not pay sufficient attention to the knowledge acquired in the past. Problems have arisen because we have disregarded basic concepts of medicine. I argue for the incorporation of the beneficial features of earlier health care into the practice of modern medicine. We should modify our current thinking by adopting an historical perspective which is tempered, in turn, by scientific assessment and by application of the risk versus benefit principle. We have disregarded these older practices because, when they were all medicine had to offer, they were often not successful. The recent medical and technical achievements have been so impressive that the older concepts have been ignored and forgotten.

It is somewhat paradoxical that Behavioral Medicine might be considered as another specialty. Behavioral Medicine draws from already established disciplines and integrates their principles. Behavioral Medicine is thus a synthesis, not a further separation. It is unfortunate that Behavioral Medicine must be labeled, since it implies the formation of another specialty. Without a distinct label, however, the issues which are the concern of Behavioral Medicine would not receive proper attention in the medical schools, in the training of new physicians and in the practice of medicine.

What is needed is a revision of medical training which incorporates the concepts of Behavioral Medicine. Many older physicians understand these principles and have been applying them. The younger physicians, however, are not being trained to adopt these concepts, partly because they cannot be easily classified into existing medical disciplines. These physicians, therefore, may never practice a form of medicine which synthesizes the new with the old. The incorporation of these principles into the practice of medicine should not be difficult. Physicians need only apply the concepts to their specific discipline. A dermatologist, a cardiologist and a surgeon can equally enhance the care of their patients by recognizing the interaction of the mind and the body; by establishing a sound doctor-patient relationship; and by weighing the risks against the benefits.

Our changing system of medical care delivery must take into account the necessity of a meaningful doctor-patient relationship. Any system which fragments this relationship is difficult to justify and will not deliver the kind of medical care people require.

However, the proper application of the principles of Behavioral Medicine also involves an understanding on the part of you, the patient. You should participate in bettering your medical care by use of these principles. Health is a two-way proposition. *It is both your responsibility and that of your physician.*

Competence, understanding, caring and ample time should be provided by a good physician. If you fail to receive this type of attention, you should seek another physician. You should not hesitate to ask what is being done to you or why it is being done. You are entitled to understand as much as possible regarding the management of your health. In rendering this information, the doctor will enhance the establishment of a sound doctor-patient relationship.

Perhaps the most important quality you should sense in a physician is that the physician cares for you. Dr. Francis Weld Peabody, the first Director of the Thorndike Memorial Laboratory of Harvard Medical School, wrote in his 1927 medical classic, *The Care of the Patient:* "One of the essential qualities of the clinician is interest in humanity, for the secret of the care of the patient is in caring for the patient." Kübler-Ross quotes a student nurse who had a terminal disease. The student nurse expressed beautifully the importance of the quality of caring in a physician. She also verbalized her awareness of the doctor's emotional difficulty in coping with her forthcoming death: "I know you feel insecure, don't know what to say, don't know what to do. But please believe me, if you care, you can't go wrong. Just admit that you care. That is really for what we search . . ."

Good physicians recognize that more risk is often entailed by giving a drug than by not prescribing it. You should not always expect a prescription at the end of a visit to a doctor. Sir William Osler, the first Professor of Medicine at Johns Hopkins Medical School and a unique teacher and clinician, said: "One of the first duties of the physician is to educate . . . [people] not to take medicine." You should not assume a physician is inadequate if he does not give a prescription at the end of your visit.

You should be cautious of physicians who routinely give injections instead of oral medications. There are few circumstances outside of the hospital setting in which the injection of a drug that could be given orally is warranted. This does not include most immunizations, administration of insulin or injections directly into diseased areas of the body. Physicians who give injections instead of oral medications make ill use of the placebo effect. An injection is expected to be a potent and useful therapy. A drug administered by injection acts faster, but the effects are of a shorter duration than those of a drug taken by mouth. The risk of adverse reactions from injections is increased, since a substance which is injected may enter the blood stream directly, without first being properly modified by the filtering organs.

It is important to realize that health and disease are not distinct entities. Health represents a continuum with many variations; a state of "perfect health" does not exist. When your bodily systems are functioning adequately, you are considered healthy. Natural biological fluctuations occur and do not indicate poor health. A small change in the focusing ability of the eyes which may require corrective lenses is an impairment but does not constitute ill health. Your integrated bodily systems change continuously in response to your internal and external environments. When these adjustments are inadequate or fail to occur so that your normal ability to function is compromised, you are not healthy. It is your responsibility to understand that this continuum of health exists. Therefore, it is not reasonable to expect "perfect" functioning. You will only be disappointed. However, recognition that relatively minor variations of health are the expected state and do not normally require medical attention will enhance your state of health. You should not expect to maintain indefinitely the sense of physical well-being of a healthy young person. Such an attitude is unrealistic and likely to create many problems.

Commercial interests capitalize upon people's expectations of perpetual health. The exploitation of these expectations creates a market for products which are not only useless and costly but also carry risks. The perception of pain in one's joints, muscles or head has become a target of many different pills. People have been victimized by advertising campaigns which make them so aware of normal bodily sensations that drugs are bought to alleviate these "symptoms." You should not allow commercial interests to define your health.

Cancer has terrified people ever since it has been recognized as a disease which is associated with pain, disfigurement and death. This fear has been exploited by promoters of various fraudulent cures. Although we do not fully understand the development of cancer, we have been able to identify certain cancer-causing agents. Substantial evidence has been accumulated which links the use of tobacco to cancer. The risk of developing cancer from smoking far outweighs the risk of developing cancer from products such as certain artificial sweeteners, food colorings and flavor additives. We debate the banning of substances of minimal risk while we continue to allow the marketing of a product of excessive risk. Commercial advertising applies a knowledge of human behavior to successfully sell noxious substances. This same understanding of human behavior should be employed to influence people against the use of dangerous products.

Many of the principles of Behavioral Medicine that are not widely employed in the practice of medicine have been incorporated into what are currently referred to as "self-help" books. These books instruct people how to deal with their problems. A self-help book that utilizes the factors inherent in a positive placebo effect is often very successful. The authors establish rapport with the reader, instilling faith or trust in their advice. This trust may lead to an alteration of specific behaviors and induce a sense of well-being. There has been a proliferation of various cults and organizations that offer approaches and techniques to people seeking help and advice. The success of these books, cults and organizations indicates that the health concerns of people are not being met by our current system of medical care.

Since organized medicine does not pay sufficient attention to these health concerns, a void has been created. People will continue to seek help elsewhere and may resort to dangerous or inappropriate health practices. People will become further estranged from their doctors. They will become increasingly susceptible to those who prey upon their fears and expectations, which may have been created for exploitation.

Behavioral approaches should be employed for disorders that are behaviorally induced. A person who is deprived of sleep and subject to excessive stress sometimes develops frequent premature ventricular contractions. Although this irregularity generally does not indicate underlying disease, the condition can be disquieting. The initial therapy for these irregular heartbeats should be behavioral. The person should sleep more and try to reduce the amount of stress he or she is experiencing. Although a pharmacological approach is beneficial in reducing the premature ventricular contractions, recognition of the associated behavioral factors may eliminate the problem itself. This condition frequently occurs in young doctors during the difficult year of medical internship, when they may be required to work between ninety and one hundred hours a week. These irregular heartbeats spontaneously disappear when the number of working hours is decreased.

When you suffer from a disease whose development is unrelated to behavioral factors, appendicitis for example, behavioral considerations have less import. Although a good surgeon will establish a sound doctor-patient relationship that will probably aid in recovery, the surgery performed is far more important than are the nonspecific treatment factors. Similarly, if you contract an infectious disease such as bacterial pneumonia, an antibiotic is crucial. If your heart is not functioning properly, as in the case of congestive heart failure, there is no adequate substitute for the drug digitalis.

Very often a conservative approach to illness is advantageous, since fewer risks are entailed. New procedures and tests can sometimes establish a diagnosis that would not previously have been possible. This may lead to the earlier initiation of proper treatment. However, it is foolish to use many tests and procedures when not necessary. Diagnostic or surgical procedures associated with a relatively large risk should not be quickly prescribed when there is time for consultation. Good physicians are receptive to the opinions of other physicians.

Popular, new therapies or diagnostic procedures should be questioned if there is a risk involved. With most new therapies and procedures, there is a considerable placebo effect, since there are favorable expectations on both the part of the physician and the patient. In many instances the adverse side effects have not yet been recognized. The nineteenth-century French physician, Armand Trousseau, understood this phenomenon. The following statement is generally attributed to him: "You should treat as many patients as possible with the new drugs while they still have the power to heal."

Modern medicine cannot cure all pains and diseases. You have the responsibility of not allowing unrealistic expectations to develop. Do not expect your physician always to know what is wrong with you. Very often an ailment does not conform with what is presently known about various diseases.

If you feel well, it is generally not necessary for you to see a physician. Indeed, the worth of the annual physical examination has recently been questioned. However, the course of certain diseases, such as hypertension, glaucoma and some types of cancer, can be favorably altered if they are detected early. Further, routine contact with a physician does much to enhance a positive placebo effect. The reassurance itself is worthwhile. A physician need only take a thorough medical history and perform a short physical examination to achieve these benefits. Blood tests and x-rays are not warranted on an annual basis in a healthy individual. They are not only expensive, but their risks outweigh their benefits. You should not expose yourself to diagnostic and therapeutic situations in which a standardized set of "shotgun"

laboratory tests and procedures are performed before a physician takes a medical history. Laboratory
tests and procedures should be used judiciously and
ordered on the basis of what has been learned from
the medical history. Otherwise, the tests are comparable to a fishing expedition.

Further, the results generated by the sophisticated
new technologies are frequently difficult to translate
into appropriate therapies. If you undergo Holter-
monitoring or exercise-testing as part of a routine
physical examination and occasional irregular heartbeats are noted, should they be treated? Since
"normal" limits have not yet been established for the
results produced by these new technologies, the
relative risks and benefits of therapy cannot be
assessed. Often you will be left only with the nagging
thought that there is "something wrong" with you,
when indeed the "irregularity" might simply be a
normal variation of your own daily physiology. If
you are ill, extensive tests and procedures may be
required to diagnose and treat your ailment. However, even then the risk versus benefit principle
should be applied.

You should not allow yourself to become convinced that you are sick or becoming sick. Is it not
foolish to spend healthy years worried about disease
that is not present and may never occur? Many individuals in previous generations appeared to have
faith in their own health. People should strive to
adopt this attitude. If you become ill, the medical
profession is there to help you. There will be enough

time for you to work with your physician and to learn how to adjust to an illness if it occurs.

If you expect everlasting youth and try to attain it, you will probably cause yourself anxiety and physical harm. You have a right to expect to be as well as possible for as long as possible. You and the medical profession working together can achieve a proper balance of old and new medical practices and bring this expectation closer to realization.

SOURCES

FOREWORD

May, H. G., and B. M. Metzger (eds.). *The New Oxford Annotated Bible*. New York: Oxford University Press, 1973.

Schwartz, G. E., and S. M. Weiss. What is behavioral medicine? *Psychosomatic Medicine* 39:377–81, 1977.

CHAPTER 1

Huang Ti Nei Ching Su Wen. *The Yellow Emperor's Classic of Internal Medicine*. Translated by Ilza Veith. Berkeley: University of California Press, 1966.

CHAPTER 2

Barker, J. C. Angor Animi. *British Medical Journal* 2:688, 1964.

Basedow, H. *The Australian Aboriginal*. Cited by W. B. Cannon in "Voodoo" death.

Blank, H., and M. W. Brody. Recurrent herpes simplex. *Psychosomatic Medicine* 12:254–60, 1950.

Calder, N. *The Mind of Man.* New York: Viking Press, 1970.

Cannon, W. B. "Voodoo" death. *American Anthropologist* 44:169–81, 1942.

Coolidge, J. C. Unexpected death in a patient who wished to die. *Journal of the American Psychoanalytic Association* 17:413–20, 1969.

Descartes, R. *The Philosophical Works of Descartes.* Vol. 1. Translated by E. S. Haldane and G. R. T. Ross. New York: Cambridge University Press, 1972.

Engel, G. L. A life setting conducive to illness. *Bulletin of the Menninger Clinic* 32:355–65, 1968.

———. Sudden and rapid death during psychological stress. *Annals of Internal Medicine* 74:771–82, 1971.

Frank, J. D. Psychiatry, the healthy individual. *American Journal of Psychiatry* 134:1349–55, 1977.

Gutmann, M. C., and H. Benson. Interaction of environmental factors and systemic arterial blood pressure: A review. *Medicine* 50:543–53, 1971.

Heilig, R., and H. Hoff. Über psychogene Entstehung des Herpes labialis. *Medizinische Klinik* 24:1472, 1928.

Holmes, T. H., and R. H. Rahe. The social readjustment rating scale. *Journal of Psychosomatic Research* 11:213–18, 1967.

Laurence, J. Z. A case of sudden death without any adequate postmortem experience. *British Medical Journal* i:376, 1860. Cited by N. R. Shulack in Sudden "exhaustive" death in excited patients.

Lown, B., J. V. Temte, P. Reich, C. Gaughan, Q. Regestein and H. Hai. Basis for recurring ventricular fibrillation in the absence of coronary heart disease and its management. *New England Journal of Medicine* 294:623–29, 1976.

Lown, B., R. L. Verrier and S. H. Rabinowitz. Neural and psychologic mechanisms and the problem of sudden cardiac death. *American Journal of Cardiology* 39:890–901, 1977.

Mathis, J. L. A sophisticated version of voodoo death: Report of a case. *Psychosomatic Medicine* 26:104–7, 1964.

May, H. G., and B. M. Metzger (eds.). *The New Oxford Annotated Bible.* New York: Oxford University Press, 1973.

Meinhardt, K., and H. A. Robinson. Stokes-Adams syndrome precipitated by emotional stress. *Psychosomatic Medicine* 24:325–30, 1962.

Menninger von Lerchenthal, E. Death from psychic causes. *Bulletin of the Menninger Clinic* 12:31–36, 1948.

Milton, G. W. Self-willed death or the bone-pointing syndrome. *Lancet* i:1435–36, 1973.

Moritz, A. R., and N. Zamcheck. Sudden and unexpected deaths of young soldiers. *Archives of Pathology* 42:459–94, 1946.

Richter, C. P. On the phenomenon of sudden death in animals and man. *Psychosomatic Medicine* 19:191–98, 1957.

Rosellini, R. A., Y. M. Binik and M. E. P. Seligman. Sudden death in the laboratory rat. *Psychosomatic Medicine* 38:55–58, 1976.

Saul, L. J. Sudden death at impasse. *Psychoanalytic Forum* 1:88–89, 1966.

Schneck, J. M. The psychological component in a case of herpes simplex. *Psychosomatic Medicine* 9:62–64, 1947.

Schultz, D. *A History of Modern Psychology.* New York: Academic Press, 1975.

Shulack, N. R. Sudden "exhaustive" death in excited patients. *Psychiatric Quarterly* 18:3–12, 1944.

Sigler, L. H. Emotion and atherosclerotic heart disease. I. Electrocardiographic changes observed on the recall of past emotional disturbances. *British Journal of Medical Psychology* 40:55–64, 1967.

CHAPTER 3

Ackerknecht, E. H. *Medicine and Ethnology*. Baltimore: Johns Hopkins Press, 1971.
———. Problems of primitive medicine. *Bulletin of the History of Medicine* 11:503–21, 1942.
Benson, H., and M. D. Epstein. The placebo effect. *Journal of the American Medical Association* 232:1225–27, 1975.
Burgess, A. M., and A. M. Burgess, Jr. Caring for the patient—a thrice-told tale. *New England Journal of Medicine* 274:1241–44, 1966.
Charcot, J. M. Cited by E. H. Ackerknecht, *Medicine and Ethnology*.
Frank, J. D. Foreword. In A. Kiev (ed.), *Magic, Faith and Healing*, pp. vii–xii.
———. *Persuasion and Healing*. New York: Schocken Books, 1963.
Gelfand, M. *The African Witch*. London: E. and S. Livingstone, 1967.
———. *Medicine and Custom in Africa*. London: E. and S. Livingstone, 1964.
———. *Witch Doctor*. London: Harvill Press, 1964.
Gregg, J. Commerce of the prairies, or the journal of a Santa Fe trader. In R. G. Thwaites (ed.), *Early Western Travels, 1748–1846*, Vol. 20. Cited by V. J. Vogel in *American Indian Medicine*.
Grollig, F. X., and H. B. Haley (eds.). *Medical Anthropology*. The Hague: Mouton, 1976.
Gunn, S. W. H. Totemic medicine and shamanism among the northwest American Indians. *Journal of the American Medical Association* 196:700–6, 1966.
Harbison, S. P. Routinism, iatrogenics, and surgical care. *Journal of the Kentucky Medical Association* 63:334–37, 392, 1965.

Kiev, A. (ed.). *Magic, Faith and Healing*. London: Collier-Macmillan, 1964.

Kiteme, K. Traditional African medicine. In F. X. Grollig and H. B. Haley (eds.), *Medical Anthropology*, pp. 413–17.

Knowles, J. H. *Doing Better and Feeling Worse*. New York: W. W. Norton, 1977.

Lesse, S. Placebo reactions in psychotherapy. *Diseases of the Nervous System* 23:313–19, 1962.

Liberman, R. An analysis of the placebo phenomenon. *Journal of Chronic Diseases* 15:761–83, 1962.

Lippman, L. Let's use the placebo. *Mental Retardation* 14:25, 1976.

Lommel, A. *Shamanism: The Beginning of Art*. New York: McGraw-Hill, 1967.

McDermott, W. Evaluating the physician and his technology. In J. H. Knowles (ed.), *Doing Better and Feeling Worse*, pp. 135–57.

Mason, R. C., Jr., G. Clark, R. B. Reeves, Jr., and S. B. Wagner. Acceptance and healing. *Journal of Religion and Health* 8:123–42, 1969.

Moertel, C. G., W. F. Taylor, A. Roth and F. A. J. Tyce. Who responds to sugar pills? *Mayo Clinic Proceedings* 51:96–100, 1976.

Ndeti, K. The relevance of African traditional medicine in modern medical training and practice. In F. X. Grollig and H. B. Haley (eds.), *Medical Anthropology*, pp. 11–26.

Shapiro, A. K. Factors contributing to the placebo effect: Their implications for psychotherapy. *American Journal of Psychotherapy* 18:73–88, 1964.

———. The placebo effect in the history of medical treatment—implications for psychiatry. *American Journal of Psychiatry* 116:298–304, 1959.

Vogel, V. J. *American Indian Medicine*. Norman: University of Oklahoma Press, 1970.

Weatherhead, L. D. *Psychology, Religion and Healing*. New York: Abingdon-Cokesbury Press, 1951.

CHAPTER 4

Amery, W., and J. Dony. A clinical trial design avoiding undue placebo treatment. *Journal of Clinical Pharmacology* 15:674–79, 1975.

Beecher, H. K. Evidence for increased effectiveness of placebos with increased stress. *American Journal of Physiology* 187:163–69, 1956.

———. Increased stress and effectiveness of placebos and "active" drugs. *Science* 132:91–92, 1960.

———. The powerful placebo. *Journal of the American Medical Association* 159:1602–6, 1955.

Benson, H., and M. D. Epstein. The placebo effect. *Journal of the American Medical Association* 232: 1225–27, 1975.

Bogdanoff, M. D., C. R. Nichols, R. F. Klein and C. Eisdorfer. The doctor-patient relationship. *Journal of the American Medical Association* 192:45–48, 1965.

Burgess, A. M., and A. M. Burgess, Jr. Caring for the patient—a thrice-told tale. *New England Journal of Medicine* 274:1241–44, 1966.

Cheek, D. B. What does the surgically anesthetized patient hear? *Rocky Mountain Medical Journal* 57:49–53, 1960.

Chessick, R. D., R. L. McFarland, R. K. Clark, M. Hammer and M. I. Bassan. The effect of morphine, chlorpromazine, pentobarbital, and placebo on anxiety. *Journal of Nervous and Mental Diseases* 141:540–48, 1966.

Corney, R. T. Iatrogenic emotional reactions. *Virginia Medical Monthly* 96:666–69, 1969.

Davidson, J. N. G. Iatrogenic psychosomatic illness or neuroses of our own doing. *New Zealand Medical Journal* 66:98–102, 1967.

Dinnerstein, A. J., and J. Halm. Modification of placebo effects by means of drugs: Effects of aspirin and placebos on self-rated moods. *Journal of Abnormal Psychology* 75:308–14, 1970.

Dorland's Illustrated Medical Dictionary. 25th ed. Philadelphia: W. B. Saunders, 1974.

Fischer, H. K., and B. M. Dlin. The dynamics of placebo therapy: A clinical study. *American Journal of Medical Science* 232:504–12, 1956.

Forrer, G. R. Psychoanalytic theory of placebo. *Diseases of the Nervous System* 25:655–61, 1964.

Freedman, N., D. M. Engelhardt, L. D. Hankoff, B. S. Glick, H. Kaye, J. Buchwald and P. Stark. Drop-out from outpatient psychiatric treatment. *Archives of Neurology and Psychiatry* 80:657–66, 1958.

Gliedman, L. H., W. H. Gantt and H. A. Teitelbaum. Some implications of conditional reflex studies for placebo research. *American Journal of Psychiatry* 113:1103–7, 1954.

Hankoff, L. D., D. M. Engelhardt and N. Freedman. Placebo response in schizophrenic outpatients. *Archives of General Psychiatry* 2:43–52, 1960.

Hippocrates, *Precepts,* Chap. 6. Cited by A. M. Burgess and A. M. Burgess, Jr., in Caring for the patient— a thrice-told tale.

Kast, E. C., and J. Loesch. A contribution to the methodology of clinical appraisal of drug action. *Psychosomatic Medicine* 21:228–34, 1959.

Kelman, H. C. Human use of human subjects: The problem of deception in social psychological experiments. *Psychological Bulletin* 67:1–11, 1967.

Klerman, G. L. Assessing the influence of the hospital milieu upon the effectiveness of psychiatric drug therapy: Problems of conceptualization and of research methodology. *Journal of Nervous and Mental Diseases* 137:143–54, 1963.

Lesse, S. Placebo reactions in psychotherapy. *Diseases of the Nervous System* 23:313–19, 1962.

Liberman, R. An analysis of the placebo phenomenon. *Journal of Chronic Diseases* 15:761–83, 1962.

167

Moertel, C. G., W. F. Taylor, A. Roth and F. A. J. Tyce. Who responds to sugar pills? *Mayo Clinic Proceedings* 51:96–100, 1976.

Nash, E. H., J. D. Frank, S. D. Imber and A. R. Stone. Selected effects of inert medication on psychiatric outpatients. *American Journal of Psychotherapy* 18:33–48, 1964.

Rashkis, H. A., and E. R. Smarr. Psychopharmacotherapeutic research: A triadistic approach. *Archives of Neurology and Psychiatry* 77:202–9, 1957.

Roethlisberger, F. J., and W. J. Dickson. *Management and the Worker.* Cambridge, Mass.: Harvard University Press, 1961.

Rosenthal, D., and J. D. Frank. Psychotherapy and the placebo effect. *Psychological Bulletin* 53:294–301, 1956.

Shapiro, A. K. Factors contributing to the placebo effect: Their implications for psychotherapy. *American Journal of Psychotherapy* 18:73–88, 1964.

———. Placebo effects in psychotherapy and psychoanalysis. *Journal of Clinical Pharmacology* 10:73–78, 1970.

Spain, D. M. (ed.). *The Complications of Modern Medical Practices.* New York: Grune and Stratton, 1963.

Tamerin, J. S., and J. F. Scavetta. Iatrogenic depression. *Journal of the American Medical Association* 219:375–76, 1972.

Von Felsinger, J. M., L. Lasagna and H. K. Beecher. Drug-induced mood changes in man: 2. Personality and reactions to drugs. *Journal of the American Medical Association* 157:1113–19, 1955.

Warshaw, L. J. Toxicity following the use of placebos. In D. M. Spain (ed.), *The Complications of Modern Medical Practices,* pp. 300–13.

Wheatley, D. Influence of doctors' and patients' attitudes in the treatment of neurotic illness. *Lancet* ii:1133–35, 1967.

Wolf, S. Effects of suggestion and conditioning on the action of chemical agents in human subjects: The pharmacology of placebos. *Journal of Clinical Investigation* 29:100–9, 1950.

Wolf, S., and R. H. Pinsky. Effects of placebo administration and occurrence of toxic reactions. *Journal of the American Medical Association* 155:339–41, 1954.

CHAPTER 5

Artiss, K. L., and A. S. Levine. Doctor-patient relation in severe illness. *New England Journal of Medicine* 288:1210–14, 1973.

Barber, B. Compassion in medicine: Toward new definitions and new institutions. *Seminars in Medicine of the Beth Israel Hospital, Boston* 295:939–43, 1976.

Bean, W. B. *Aphorisms from Latham.* Iowa City: Prairie Press, 1962.

Bennett, I. L., Jr. Technology as a shaping force. In J. H. Knowles (ed.), *Doing Better and Feeling Worse,* pp. 125–33.

Burgess, A. M., and A. M. Burgess, Jr. Caring for the patient—a thrice-told tale. *New England Journal of Medicine* 274:1241–44, 1966.

Clark, D. W., and B. MacMahon (eds.). *Preventive Medicine.* Boston: Little, Brown, 1967.

Crawshaw, R. Humanism in medicine—the rudimentary process. *New England Journal of Medicine* 293:1320–22, 1975.

Dingle, J. H. An epidemiological study of illness in families. *The Harvey Lecture Series LIII, 1957–1958.* New York: Academic Press, 1959.

———. The ills of man. *Scientific American* 229:76–89, 1973.

Duval, M. K. The provider, the government, and the consumer. In J. H. Knowles (ed.), *Doing Better and Feeling Worse,* pp. 185–92.

169

Ebert, R. H. Medical education in the United States. In J. H. Knowles (ed.), *Doing Better and Feeling Worse*, pp. 171–84.

Eisenberg, L. The search for care. In J. H. Knowles (ed.), *Doing Better and Feeling Worse*, pp. 235–46.

Fry, J. *Profiles of Disease*. London: E. and S. Livingstone, 1966.

Garrison, F. H. *History of Medicine*. Philadelphia: W. B. Saunders, 1924.

Ginzberg, E. Health services, power centers, and decision-making mechanisms. In J. H. Knowles (ed.), *Doing Better and Feeling Worse*, pp. 203–13.

Greenblatt, R. B. *Search the Scriptures*. Philadelphia: J. B. Lippincott, 1963.

Harbison, S. P. Routinism, iatrogenics, and surgical care. *Journal of the Kentucky Medical Association* 63:334–37, 392, 1965.

Hodgkin, K. *Towards Earlier Diagnosis*. London: E. and S. Livingstone, 1963.

Klarman, H. E. The financing of health care. In J. H. Knowles (ed.), *Doing Better and Feeling Worse*, pp. 215–34.

Knowles, J. H. *Doing Better and Feeling Worse*. New York: W. W. Norton, 1977.

McDermott, W. Evaluating the physician and his technology. In J. H. Knowles (ed.), *Doing Better and Feeling Worse*, pp. 135–57.

Moore, A. R. Medical humanities—a new medical adventure. *New England Journal of Medicine* 295:1479–80, 1976.

Mueller, M. S., and R. M. Gibson. National health expenditures, fiscal year 1975. *Social Security Bulletin* 39:3–20, 48, 1976.

Paton, A. "Medicalization" of health. *British Medical Journal* 4:573–74, 1974.

Rogers, D. E. The challenge of primary care. In J. H. Knowles (ed.), *Doing Better and Feeling Worse*, pp. 81–103.

Scientific and Educational Basis for Improving Health Care: Report of the Panel on Biological and Medical Science of the President's Science Advisory Committee. Washington, D.C.: U.S. Government Printing Office, 1972. Cited by I. L. Bennett, Jr., in J. H. Knowles (ed.), *Doing Better and Feeling Worse*.

Thomas, L. Aspects of biomedical science policy: An occasional paper. Cited by I. L. Bennett, Jr., in J. H. Knowles (ed.), *Doing Better and Feeling Worse*.

————. Biostatistics in medicine. *Science* 198:675, 1977.

————. *The Lives of a Cell*. New York: Viking Press, 1974.

————. On the science and technology of medicine. In J. H. Knowles (ed.), *Doing Better and Feeling Worse*, pp. 35–46.

U.S. Bureau of the Census, *Statistical Abstract of the United States: 1977* (98th ed.). Washington, D.C., 1977.

Wechsler, H. *Handbook of Medical Specialties*. New York: Human Sciences Press, 1976.

Werner, A., and J. M. Schneider. Teaching medical students interactional skills. *New England Journal of Medicine* 290:1232–37, 1974.

White, K. L. Patterns of medical practice. In D. W. Clark and B. MacMahon (eds.), *Preventive Medicine*, pp. 849–70.

Willius, F. A. *Aphorisms of Dr. Charles Horace Mayo and Dr. William James Mayo*. Rochester, Minn.: Whiting Press, 1951.

CHAPTER 6

Adams, D. F., D. B. Fraser and H. L. Abrams. The complications of coronary arteriography. *Circulation* 48:609–18, 1973.

Almy, T. P. Meditation on a forest path. *New England Journal of Medicine* 297:165–67, 1977.

Anonymous. Who and what. *Pediatrics* 55:753–55, 1975.

Aronow, W. S., W. H. Allen, D. De Cristofaro and S. Ungermann. Follow-up of mass screening for coronary risk factors in 1817 adults. *Circulation* 51:1038–45, 1975.

Barnes, M. L. Commentary on iatrogenic disease. *Annals of Clinical and Laboratory Science* 6:278–82, 1976.

Bean, W. B. *Aphorisms from Latham.* Iowa City: Prairie Press, 1962.

Beaty, H. N., and R. G. Petersdorf. Iatrogenic factors in infectious disease. *Annals of Internal Medicine* 65: 641–56, 1966.

Benson, H. Systemic hypertension and the relaxation response. *New England Journal of Medicine* 296:1152–56, 1977.

Benson, H., J. B. Kotch and K. D. Crassweller. Stress and hypertension: Interrelations and management. In G. Onesti and A. M. Brest (eds.), *Hypertension: Mechanisms, Diagnosis and Treatment,* pp. 113–24.

Burgess, A. M. and A. M. Burgess, Jr. Caring for the patient—a thrice-told tale. *New England Journal of Medicine* 274:1241–44, 1966.

Camilleri, A. P. Iatrogenic disease in obstetrics and gynaecology. *Practitioner* 204:406–11, 1970.

Cluff, L. E., G. F. Thornton and L. G. Seidl. Studies on the epidemiology of adverse drug reactions. I. Method of surveillance. *Journal of the American Medical Association* 188:976–83, 1964.

Dorland's Illustrated Medical Dictionary. 25th ed. Philadelphia: W. B. Saunders, 1974.

Duma, R. J. First of all do no harm. *New England Journal of Medicine* 285:1258–59, 1971.

Editorial. Diseases of medical progress. *Southern Medical Journal* 59:871–72, 1966.

———. A cure for iatrogenic disease: Look before you leap. *Geriatrics* 28:56, 58, 60, 62, 1973.

Gunderson, E. K. E., and R. H. Rahe (eds.). *Life Stress and Illness.* Springfield, Ill.: Charles C Thomas, 1974.

Gutmann, M. C., and H. Benson. Interaction of environmental factors and systemic arterial blood pressure: A review. *Medicine* 50:543–53, 1971.

Gwynne, J. F. Iatrogenic drug damage: A review. *New Zealand Medical Journal* 75:211–14, 1972.

Hansing, C. E., K. Hammermeister, K. Prindle, R. Twiss, R. R. Schwindt, B. Gowing, L. Crecelaius and W. Robinson. Cardiac catheterization experience in hospitals without cardiovascular surgery programs. *Catheterization and Cardiovascular Diagnosis* 3:207–14, 1977.

Harbison, S. P. Routinism, iatrogenics, and surgical care. *Journal of the Kentucky Medical Association* 63:334–37, 392, 1965.

Hoddinott, B. C., C. W. Gowdey, W. K. Coulter and J. M. Parker. Drug reactions and errors in administration on a medical ward. *Canadian Medical Association Journal* 97:1001–6, 1967.

Holmes, O. W. *The Works of Oliver Wendell Holmes.* Vol. 9. *Medical Essays.* Boston: Houghton, Mifflin, 1892.

Hurwitz, N. Admissions to hospital due to drugs. *British Medical Journal* 1:539–40, 1969.

———. Predisposing factors in adverse reactions to drugs. *British Medical Journal* 1:536–39, 1969.

Hurwitz, N., and O. L. Wade. Intensive hospital monitoring of adverse reactions to drugs. *British Medical Journal* 1:531–36, 1969.

Illich, I. *Medical Nemesis.* London: Calder and Boyars, 1975.

Ingelfinger, F. J. The handbook of nonprescription drugs. *New England Journal of Medicine* 297:48–49, 1977.

Irey, N. S. Deaths due to adverse drug reactions. *Journal of the American Medical Association* 231:22–23, 1975.

Lasagna, L. The diseases drugs cause. *Perspectives in Biology and Medicine* 7:457–70, 1964.

Lucia, S. P. The iatrogenic diseases. *Northwest Medicine* 68:1129–32, 1969.

McLamb, J. T., and R. R. Huntley. The hazards of hospitalization. *Southern Medical Journal* 60:469–72, 1967.

Marmer, M. J. Iatrogenic complications. *International Anesthesiology Clinics* 10:51–65, 1972.

Modell, W. (ed.). *Drugs of Choice, 1966–1967*. St. Louis: C. V. Mosby, 1966.

Moser, R. H. (ed.). *Diseases of Medical Progress: A Study of Iatrogenic Disease*. 3rd ed. Springfield, Ill.: Charles C Thomas, 1969.

Mulroy, R. Iatrogenic disease in general practice: Its incidence and effects. *British Medical Journal* 2:407–10, 1973.

Norman, P. S. and L. E. Cluff. Adverse drug reactions and alternative drugs of choice. In W. Modell (ed.), *Drugs of Choice, 1966–1967*, pp. 30–47.

Onesti, G., and A. M. Brest (eds.). *Hypertension: Mechanisms, Diagnosis and Treatment*. Philadelphia: Davis, 1978.

Petersen, J., and F. Beissner (eds.). *Schillers Werke*. Nationalausgabe, Band I. Weimar: Hermann Böhlaus, 1943.

Physician's Desk Reference. 32nd ed. Oradell, New Jersey: Medical Economics Company, 1978.

Rich, N. M., R. W. Hobson and C. W. Fedde. Vascular trauma secondary to diagnostic and therapeutic procedures. *American Journal of Surgery* 128:715–21, 1974.

Rowe, W. S. Iatrogenic disease. *Medical Journal of Australia* 2:560–62, 1969.

Rudd, T. N. Prescribing methods and iatrogenic situations in old age. *Gerontologia Clinica* 14:123–28, 1972.

Schimmel, E. M. The hazards of hospitalization. *Annals of Internal Medicine* 60:100–10, 1964.

Seckler, J. G., and R. C. Spritzer. Disseminated disease of medical progress. *Archives of Internal Medicine* 117:447–50, 1966.

Seidl, L. G., G. F. Thornton and L. E. Cluff. Epidemiological studies of adverse drug reactions. *American Journal of Public Health* 55:1170–75, 1965.

Seidl, L. G., G. F. Thornton, J. W. Smith and L. E. Cluff. Studies on the epidemiology of adverse drug reactions. III. Reactions in patients on a general medical service. *Bulletin of the Johns Hopkins Hospital* 119:299–315, 1966.

Singh, M. Iatrogenic disorders of the fetus and newborn as a result of maternal medications. *Indian Pediatrics* 12:603–8, 1975.

Special Commission on Internal Pollution. Toward assessing the chemical age. *Journal of the American Medical Association* 234:507–9, 1975.

Spiro, H. M. Pain and perfectionism—the physician and the "pain patient." *New England Journal of Medicine* 294:829–30, 1976.

Steering committee approves statement on coin-operated blood pressure machines. *American Heart News* 5:3, 1978.

CHAPTER 7

Adams, J. E. Naloxone reversal of analgesia produced by brain stimulation in the human. *Pain* 2:161–66, 1976.

Anderson, D. G., J. L. Jamieson and S. C. Man. Analgesic effects of acupuncture on the pain of ice water: A double-blind study. *Canadian Journal of Psychology* 28:239–44, 1974.

Andersson, S. A., and E. Holmgren. On acupuncture analgesia and the mechanism of pain. *American Journal of Chinese Medicine* 3:311–34, 1975.

Anonymous. The jubilee of anesthesia. Cited by D. De Moulin in A historical-phenomenological study of bodily pain in Western man.

Arias, A. (ed.). *Recent Progress in Anaesthesiology and Resuscitation.* Amsterdam: Excerpta Medica, 1975.

Barber, T. X. The effects of "hypnosis" on pain. *Psychosomatic Medicine* 25:303–33, 1963.

Beecher, H. K. Relationship of significance of wound to pain experienced. *Journal of the American Medical Association* 161:1609–13, 1956.

Belluzzi, J. D., N. Grant, V. Garsky, D. Sarantakis, C. D. Wise and L. Stein. Analgesia induced *in vivo* by central administration of enkephalin in rat. *Nature* 260:625–26, 1976.

Berlin, F. S., R. L. Bartlett and J. D. Black. Acupuncture and placebo: Effects on delaying the terminating response to a painful stimulus. *Anesthesiology* 42:527–31, 1975.

Brunet, F. *Oeuvres médicales d'Alexandre de Tralles.* Vol. 4. Paris: Librairie Orientaliste Paul Geuthner, 1937.

Buytendijk, F. J. J. *Over de pign.* Cited by D. De Moulin in A historical-phenomenological study of bodily pain in Western man.

Castiglioni, C. *A History of Medicine.* E. B. Krumbhaar (ed.). New York: Alfred A. Knopf, 1941.

Cattell, M. The action and use of analgesics. Cited by T. X. Barber in The effects of "hypnosis" on pain.

Chapman, C. R. Psychophysical evaluation of acupuncture analgesia: Some issues and considerations. *Anesthesiology* 43:501–6, 1975.

Cohen, P. J., and R. D. Dripps. Histories and theories of general anesthesia. In L. S. Goodman and A. Gilman (eds.), *The Pharmacological Basis of Therapeutics,* pp. 42–45.

Deenadayalan, C. V. Anginal pain in a phantom limb. *British Medical Journal* 2:238, 1976.

De Moulin, D. A historical-phenomenological study of bodily pain in Western man. *Bulletin of the History of Medicine* 48:540–70, 1974.

Dioscorides. Materia medica, Lib. IV, cap. 75. Cited by D. De Moulin in A historical-phenomenological study of bodily pain in Western man.

Dupuytren, G. Cited by H. K. Beecher in Relationship of significance of wound to pain experienced.

El-Sobky, A., J. O. Dostrovsky and P. D. Wall. Lack of effect of naloxone on pain perception in humans. *Nature* 263:783–84, 1976.

Finneson, B. E. *Diagnosis and Management of Pain Syndromes.* Philadelphia: W. B. Saunders, 1969.

Galen, C. Compositiones Medicae, XI. Cited by P. Kellaway in The part played by electric fish in the early history of bioelectricity and electrotherapy.

Goodman, L. S., and A. Gilman (eds.). *The Pharmacological Basis of Therapeutics.* New York: Macmillan, 1970.

Graf, I., J. I. Szekely, A. Z. Ronai, Z. Dunai-Kovacs and S. Bajusz. B-endorphin as a potent analgesic by intravenous injection. *Nature* 263:239–41, 1976.

Hill, R. G., C. M. Pepper and J. F. Mitchell. Depression of nociceptive and other neurones in the brain by iontophoretically applied met-enkephalin. *Nature* 262:604–6, 1976.

Hughes, J., T. W. Smith, H. W. Kosterlitz, L. A. Fothergill, B. A. Morgan and H. R. Morris. Identification of two related pentapeptides from the brain with potent opiate agonist activity. *Nature* 258:577–79, 1975.

Kellaway, P. The part played by electric fish in the early history of bioelectricity and electrotherapy. *Bulletin of the History of Medicine* 20:112–37, 1946.

Kolb, L. C. *Modern Clinical Psychiatry.* Philadelphia: W. B. Saunders, 1973.

Kornetsky, C. Effects of anxiety and morphine on the anticipation and perception of painful radiant thermal stimuli. *Journal of Comparative and Physiological Psychology* 47:130–32, 1954.

Lepanto, R., W. Moroney and R. Zenhausern. The contribution of anxiety to the laboratory investigation of pain. *Psychonomic Science* 3:475, 1965.

Melzack, R. Acupuncture and pain mechanisms. In A. Arias (ed.), *Recent Progress in Anaesthesiology and Resuscitation*, pp. 27–30.

Melzack, R., and P. D. Wall. Pain mechanisms: A new theory. *Science* 150:971–79, 1965.

Plutarch. Morals, 978B. Cited by P. Kellaway in The part played by electric fish in the early history of bioelectricity and electrotherapy.

Scribonius. Cited by P. Kellaway in The part played by electric fish in the early history of bioelectricity and electrotherapy.

Secundus, C. Plinius. Historiae naturalis lib. XXXVII, Lib. 25, cap. 94. Cited by D. De Moulin in A historical-phenomenological study of bodily pain in Western man.

Seneca. Dialogorum, Lib. XII. Cited by D. De Moulin in A historical-phenomenological study of bodily pain in Western man.

Shakespeare, W. *Much Ado about Nothing*. G. L. Kittredge (ed.). Boston: Ginn and Company, 1941.

Sjolund, B., and M. Erikkson. Electro-acupuncture and endogenous morphines. *Lancet* ii:1085, 1976.

Snyder, S. H. Opiate receptors in the brain. *New England Journal of Medicine* 296:266–71, 1977.

Sternbach, R. A., and B. Tursky. Ethnic differences among housewives in psychological and skin potential responses to electric shock. *Psychophysiology* 1:241–46, 1965.

Stillings, D. A survey of the history of electrical stimulation for pain to 1900. *Medical Instrumentation* 9:255–59, 1975.

Toellner, R. Die Umbewertung des Schmerzes im 17. Jahrhundert in ihren Voraussetzungen und Folgen. Cited by D. De Moulin in A historical-phenomenological study of bodily pain in Western man.

Walker, J. M., G. G. Berntson and C. A. Sandman. An analog of enkephalin having prolonged opiate-like effects in vivo. *Science* 196:85–87, 1977.

Wesley, J. *The Desideratum: or, Electricity Made Plain and Useful.* London: W. Flexney, 1760. Cited by D. Stillings in A survey of the history of electrical stimulation for pain to 1900.

―――. *Primitive Physic.* London: John Mason, 1836.

Zborowski, M. Cultural components in responses to pain. *Journal of Social Issues* 8:16–30, 1952.

CHAPTER 8

Benson, H. *The Relaxation Response.* New York: William Morrow, 1975.

―――. Systemic hypertension and the relaxation response. *New England Journal of Medicine* 296:1152–56, 1977.

―――. Your innate asset for combatting stress. *Harvard Business Review* 52:49–60, 1974.

Benson, H., S. Alexander and C. L. Feldman. Decreased premature ventricular contractions through the use of the relaxation response in patients with stable ischemic heart disease. *Lancet* ii:380–82, 1975.

Benson, H., J. F. Beary and M. P. Carol. The relaxation response. *Psychiatry* 37:37–46, 1974.

Benson, H., and M. D. Epstein. The placebo effect—a neglected asset in the care of patients. *Journal of the American Medical Association* 232:1225–27, 1975.

Benson, H., J. B. Kotch and K. D. Crassweller. The usefulness of the relaxation response in the treatment of stress-related cardiovascular diseases. *Journal of the South Carolina Medical Association* 72:50–56, 1976.

―――. The relaxation response: A bridge between psychiatry and medicine. *Medical Clinics of North America* 61:929–38, 1977.

Benson, H., B. R. Marzetta and B. A. Rosner. Decreased blood pressure associated with the regular elicitation of the relaxation response: A study of hypertensive subjects. In R. S. Eliot (ed.), *Contemporary Problems in Cardiology*. Vol. 1. *Stress and the Heart*, pp. 293–302.

Benson, H. B., A. Rosner, B. R. Marzetta and H. Klemchuk. Decreased blood pressure in borderline hypertensive subjects who practiced meditation. *Journal of Chronic Diseases* 27:163–69, 1974.

————. Decreased blood pressure in pharmacologically treated hypertensive patients who regularly elicited the relaxation response. *Lancet* i:289–91, 1974.

Egbert, L. D., G. E. Battit, C. E. Welch and M. K. Bartlett. Reduction of postoperative pain by encouragement and instruction of patients. *New England Journal of Medicine* 270:825–27, 1964.

Eliot, R. S. (ed.). *Contemporary Problems in Cardiology*. Vol. 1. *Stress and the Heart*. Mount Kisco, N.Y.: Futura, 1974.

Gutmann, M. C., and H. Benson. Interaction of environmental factors and systemic arterial blood pressure: A review. *Medicine* 50:543–53, 1971.

Hinton, J. *Dying*. Harmondsworth, England: Penguin Books, 1972.

Holter, N. J. New method for heart studies. *Science* 134:1214–20, 1961.

Kübler-Ross, E. *Death: The Final Stage of Growth*. Englewood Cliffs, N.J.: Prentice-Hall, 1975.

————. *On Death and Dying*. New York: Macmillan, 1969.

Mount, B. M. The problem of caring for the dying in a general hospital: The palliative care unit as a possible solution. *Canadian Medical Association Journal* 115:119–21, 1976.

Peters, R. K., H. Benson and D. Porter. Daily relaxation response breaks in a working population: I. Effects on self-reported measures of health, performance, and well-being. *American Journal of Public Health* 67:946–53, 1977.

Peters, R. K., H. Benson and J. M. Peters. Daily relaxation response breaks in a working population: II. Effects on blood pressure. *American Journal of Public Health* 67:954–59, 1977.

Shephard, D. A. E. Principles and practice of palliative care. *Canadian Medical Association Journal* 116: 522–26, 1977.

Saunders, C. Cited by D. A. E. Shephard in Principles and practice of palliative care.

Voukydis, P. C., and S. A. Forwand. The effect of elicitation of the relaxation response in patients with intractable ventricular arrhythmias. *Circulation* 56:57, 1977 (Suppl. III).

Wallace, R. K., and H. Benson. The physiology of meditation. *Scientific American* 226:84–90, 1972.

Wallace, R. K., H. Benson and A. F. Wilson. A wakeful hypometabolic physiologic state. *American Journal of Physiology* 221:795–99, 1971.

Warner, G., and J. W. Lance. Relaxation therapy in migraine and chronic tension headache. *Medical Journal of Australia* 1:298–301, 1975.

CHAPTER 9

Flesch, R. (ed.). *The Book of Unusual Quotations.* London: Cassell, 1959.

Kübler-Ross, E. *Death: The Final Stage of Growth.* Englewood Cliffs, N.J.: Prentice-Hall, 1975.

Osler, W. Cited by R. Flesch (ed.) in *The Book of Unusual Quotations.*

Peabody, F. W. *The Care of the Patient.* Cambridge, Mass.: Harvard University Press, 1927.

Shapiro, A. K. A contribution to a history of the placebo effect. *Behavioral Science* 5:109–35, 1960.

Spark, R. The case against regular physicals. *New York Times Magazine* 125:10–11, 38–41, July 25, 1976.

Trousseau, A. Cited by A. K. Shapiro in A contribution to a history of the placebo effect.

INDEX

183